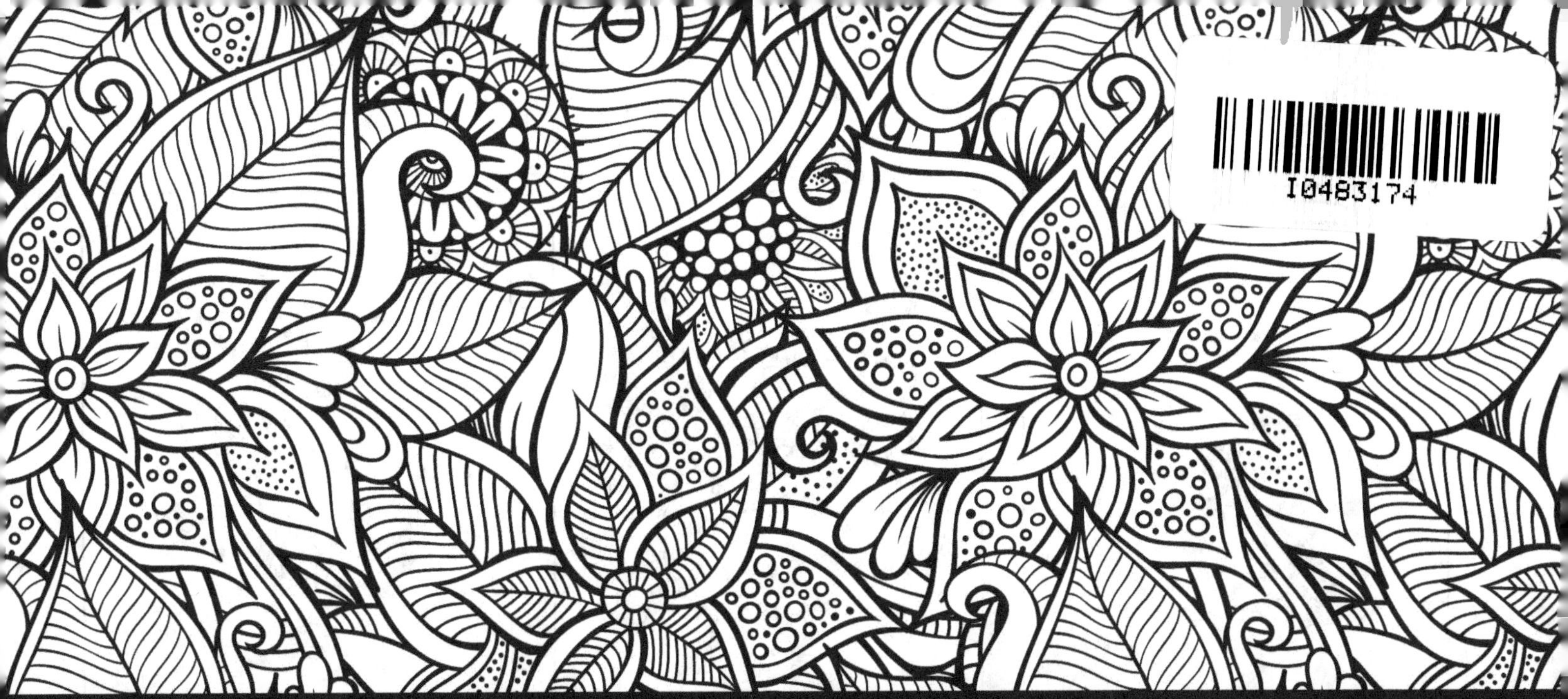

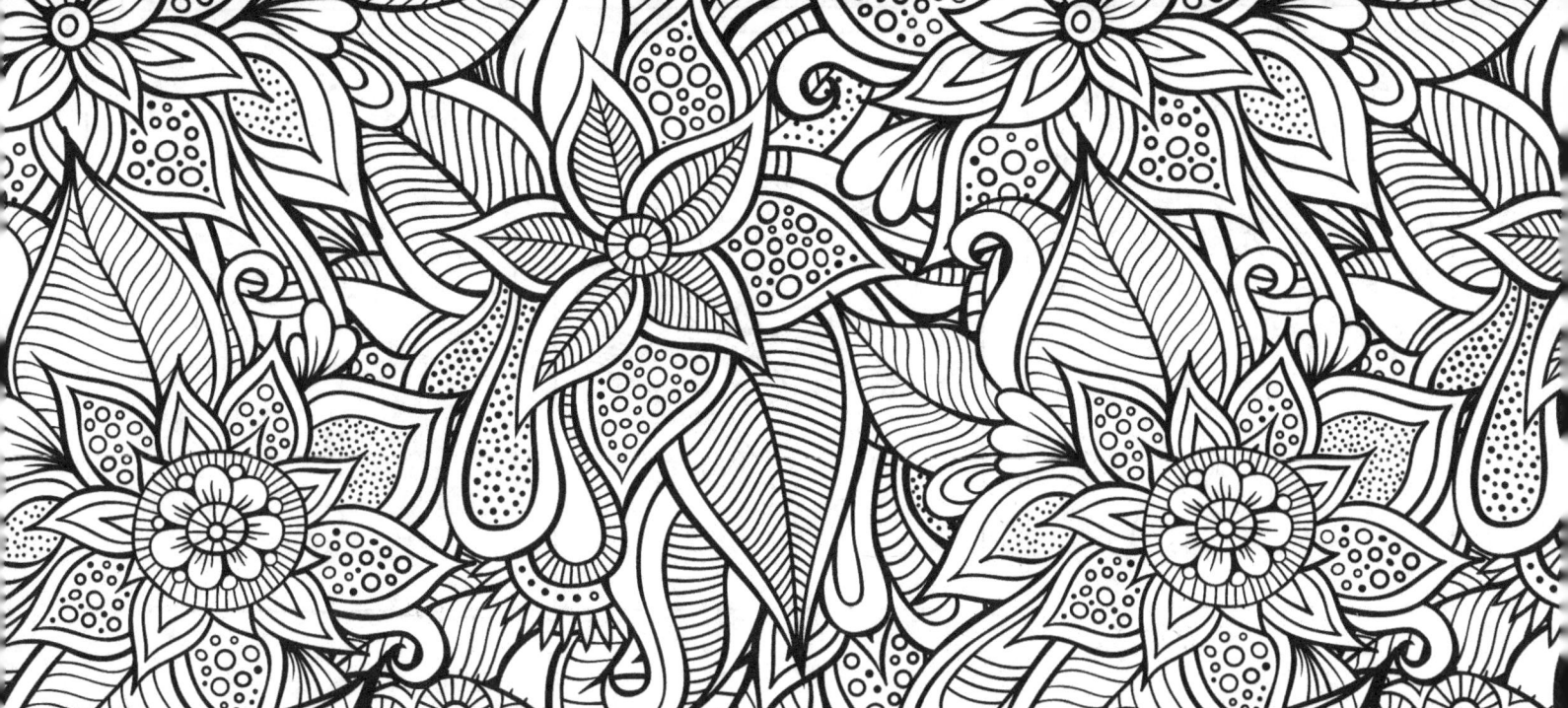

COLORING BOOKS
FOR WOMEN
RELAXING DESIGNS

▲ ART THERAPY COLORING

Preview of Coloring Pages

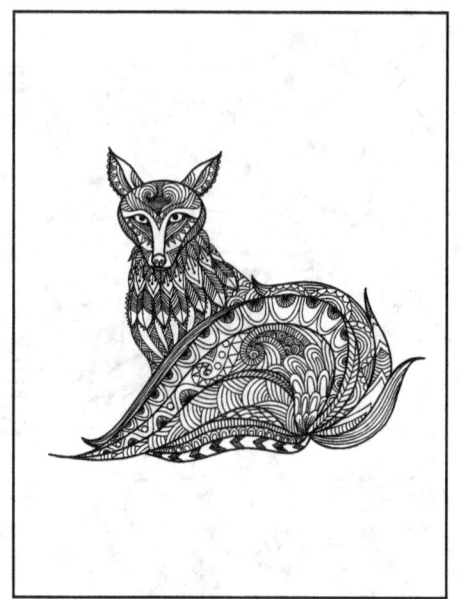
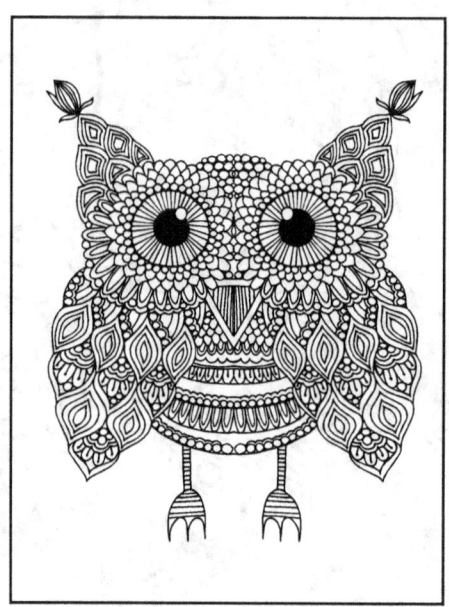
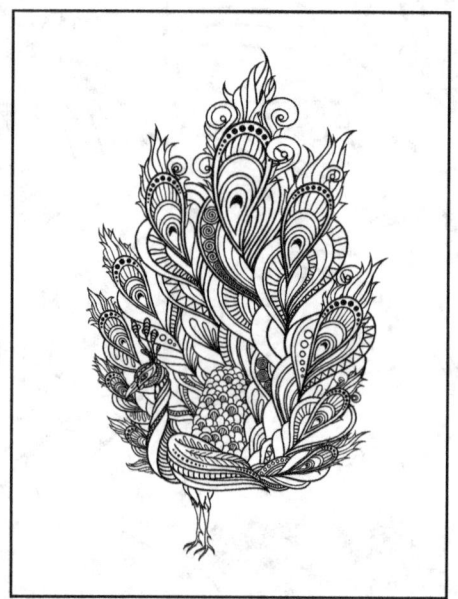
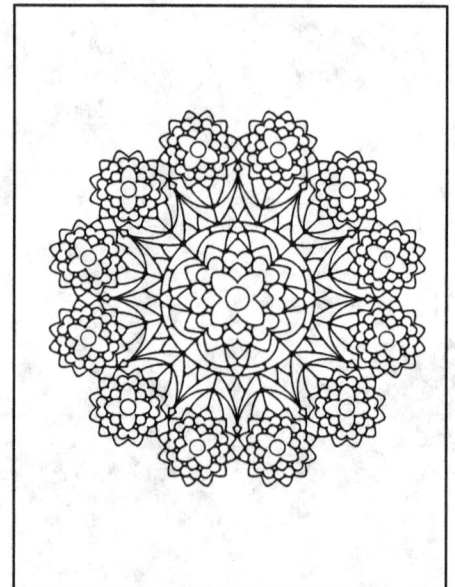
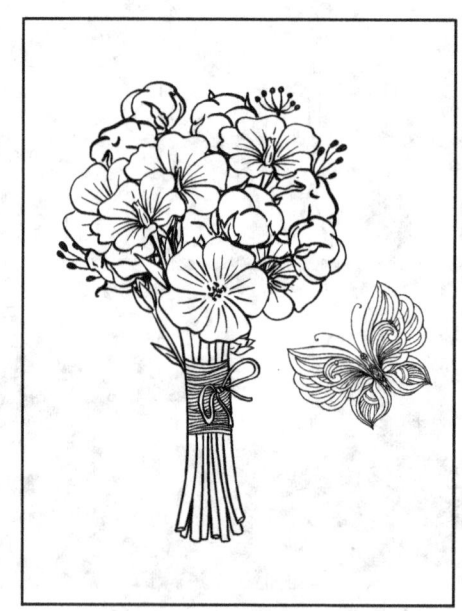
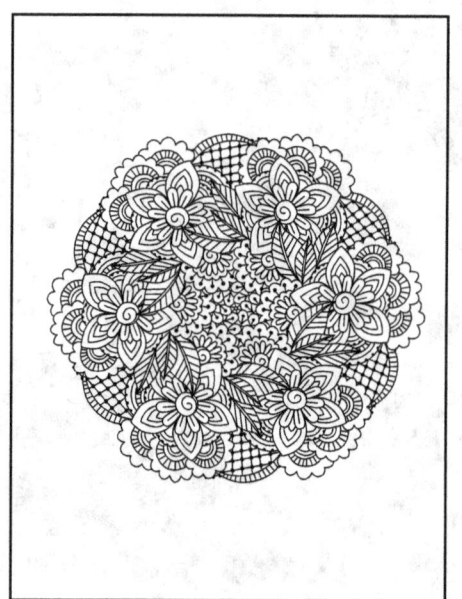
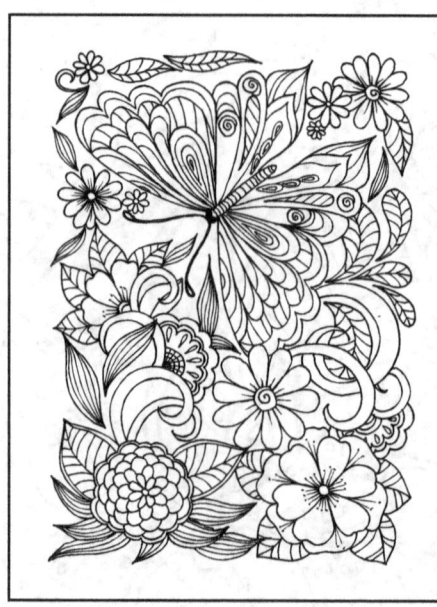
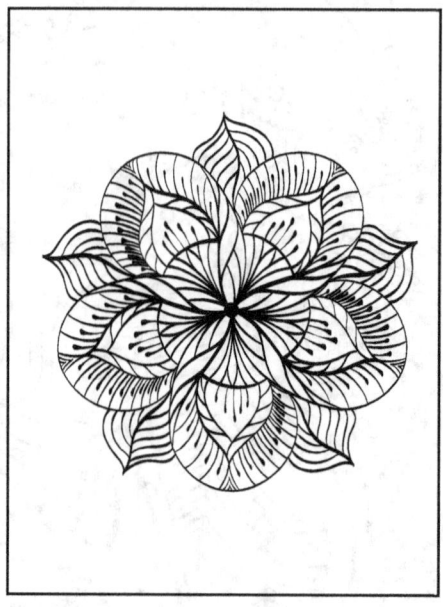
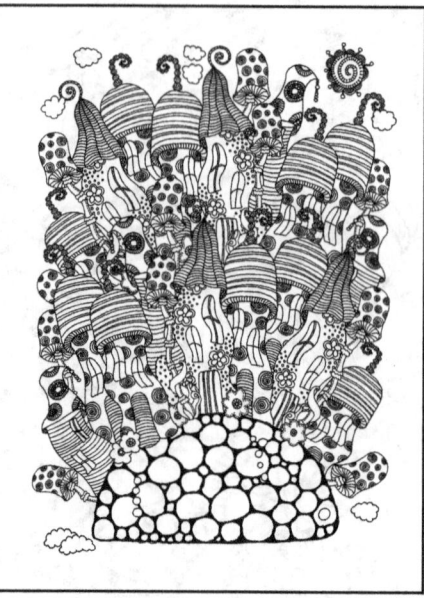

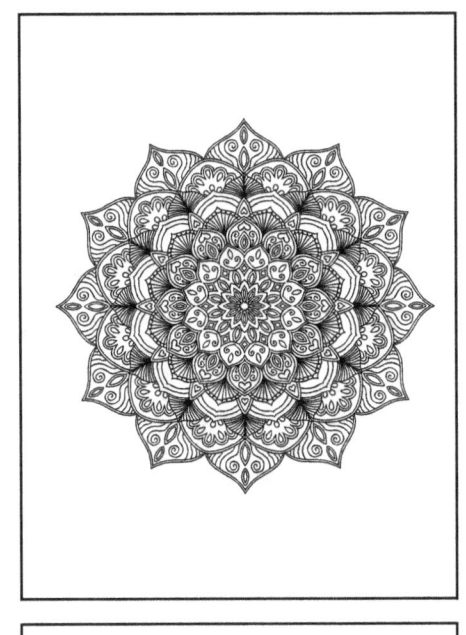
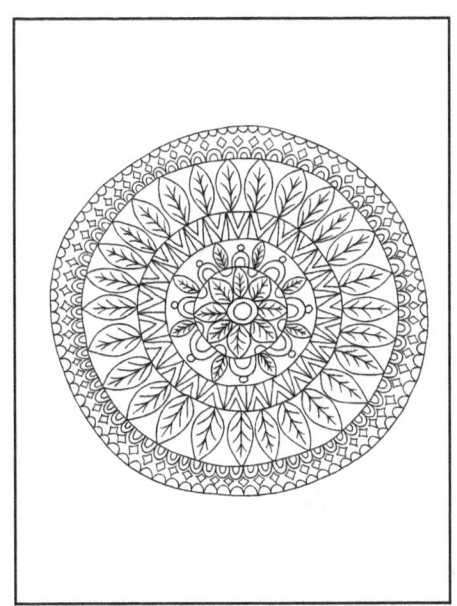
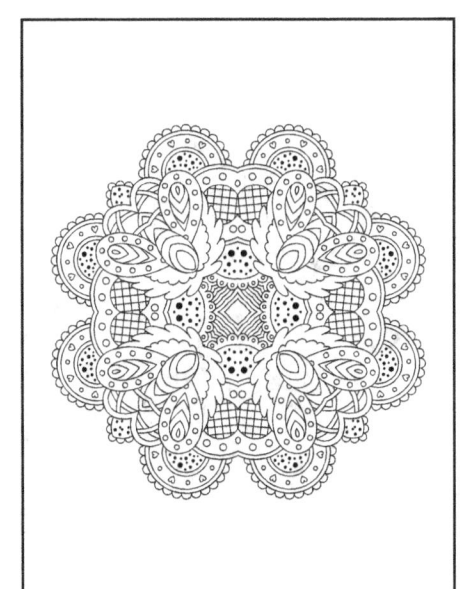
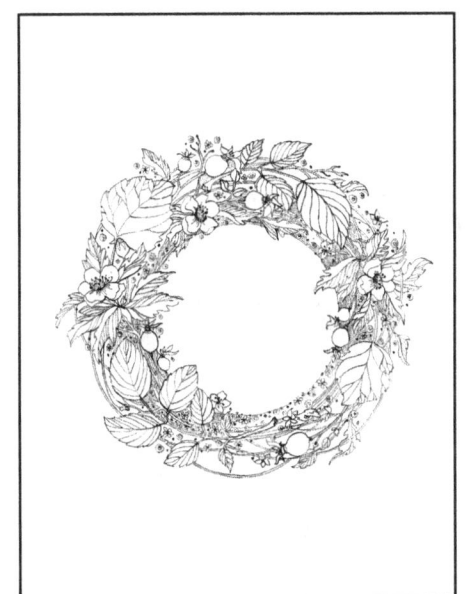
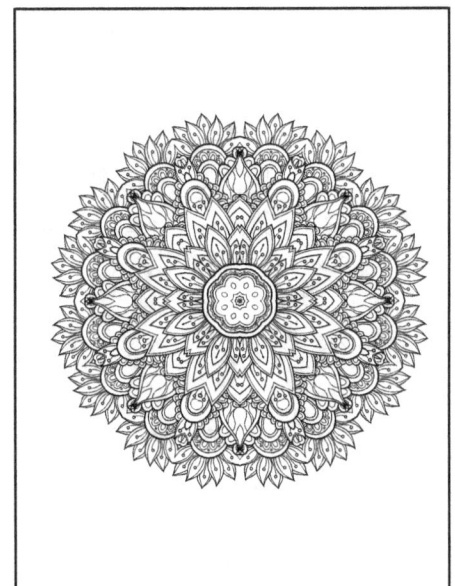
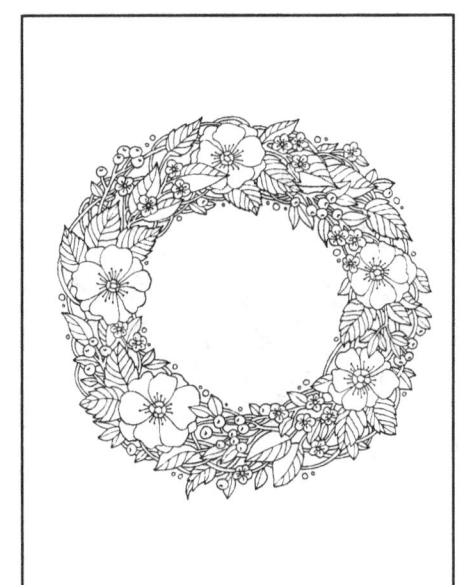
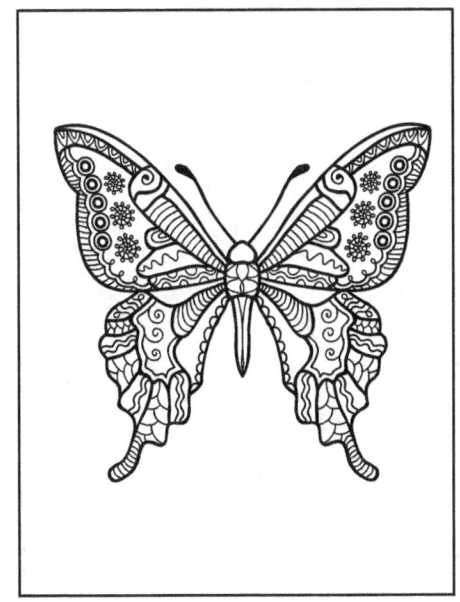
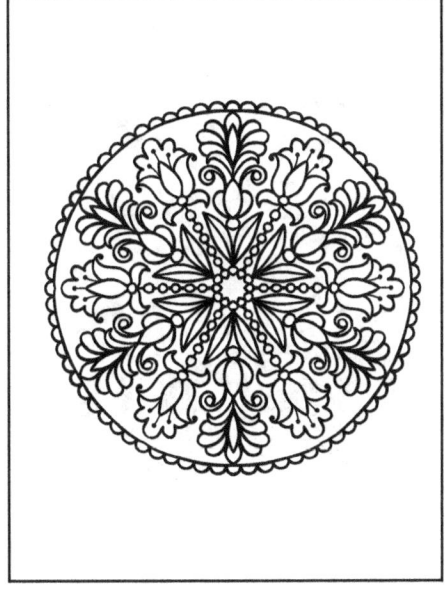
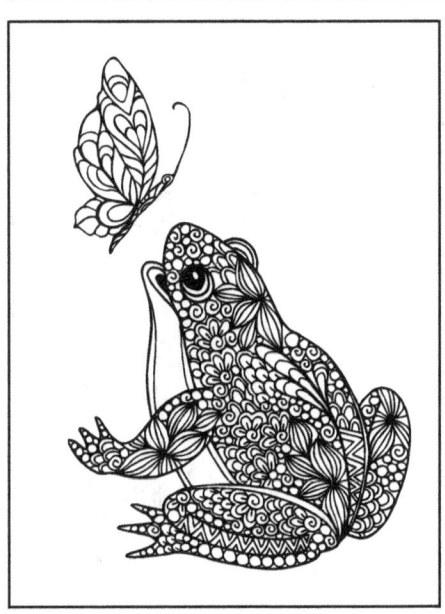

Preview of Coloring Pages

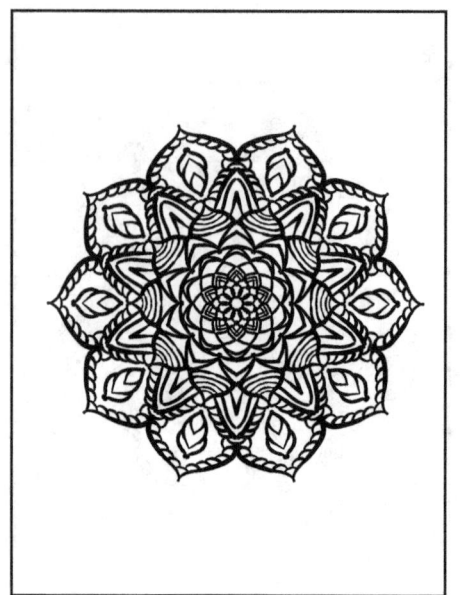
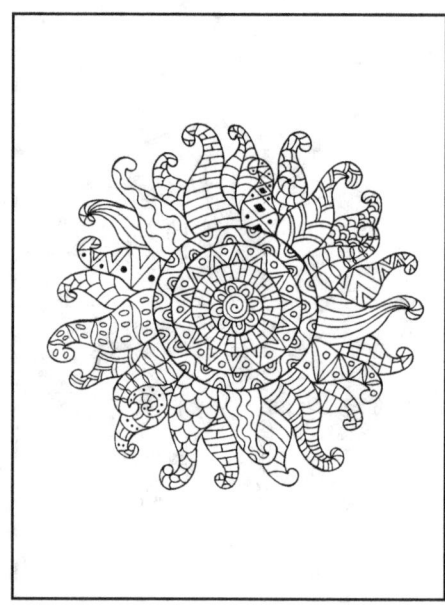
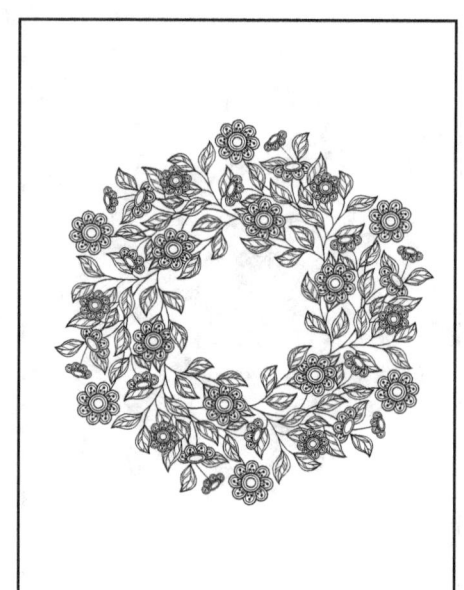
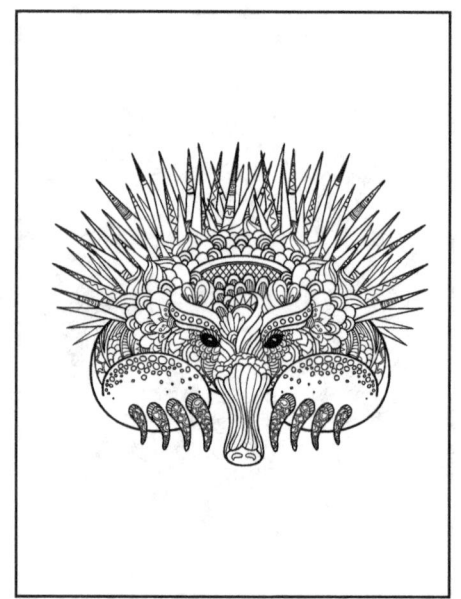
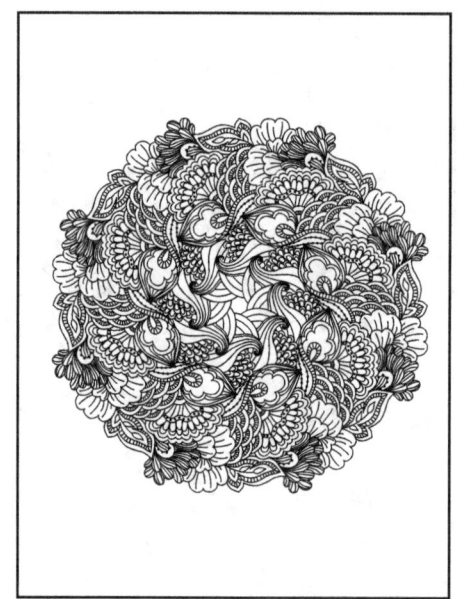
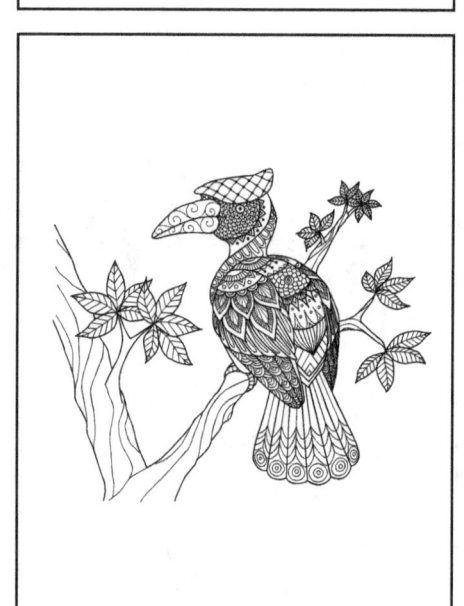
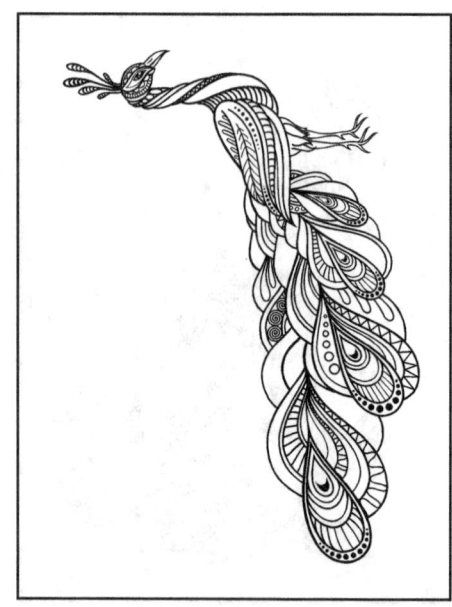
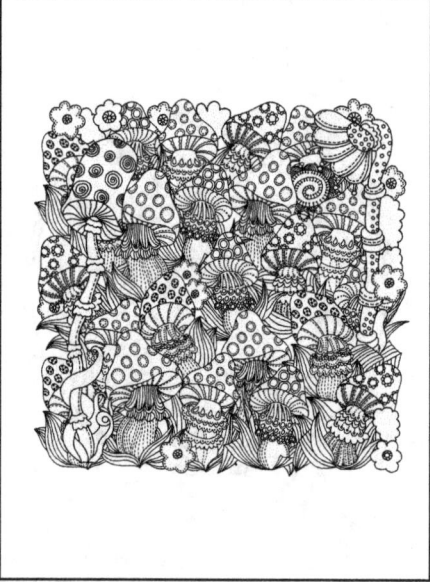
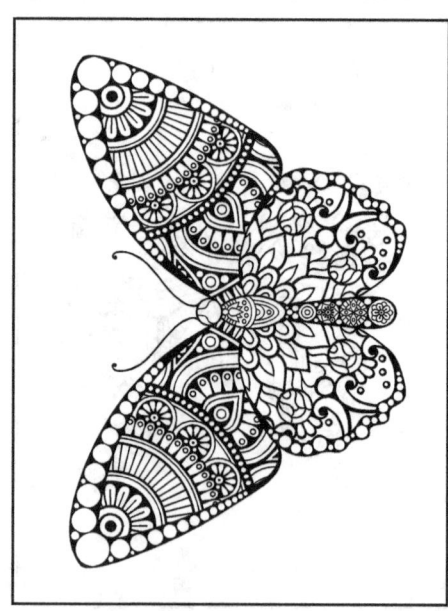

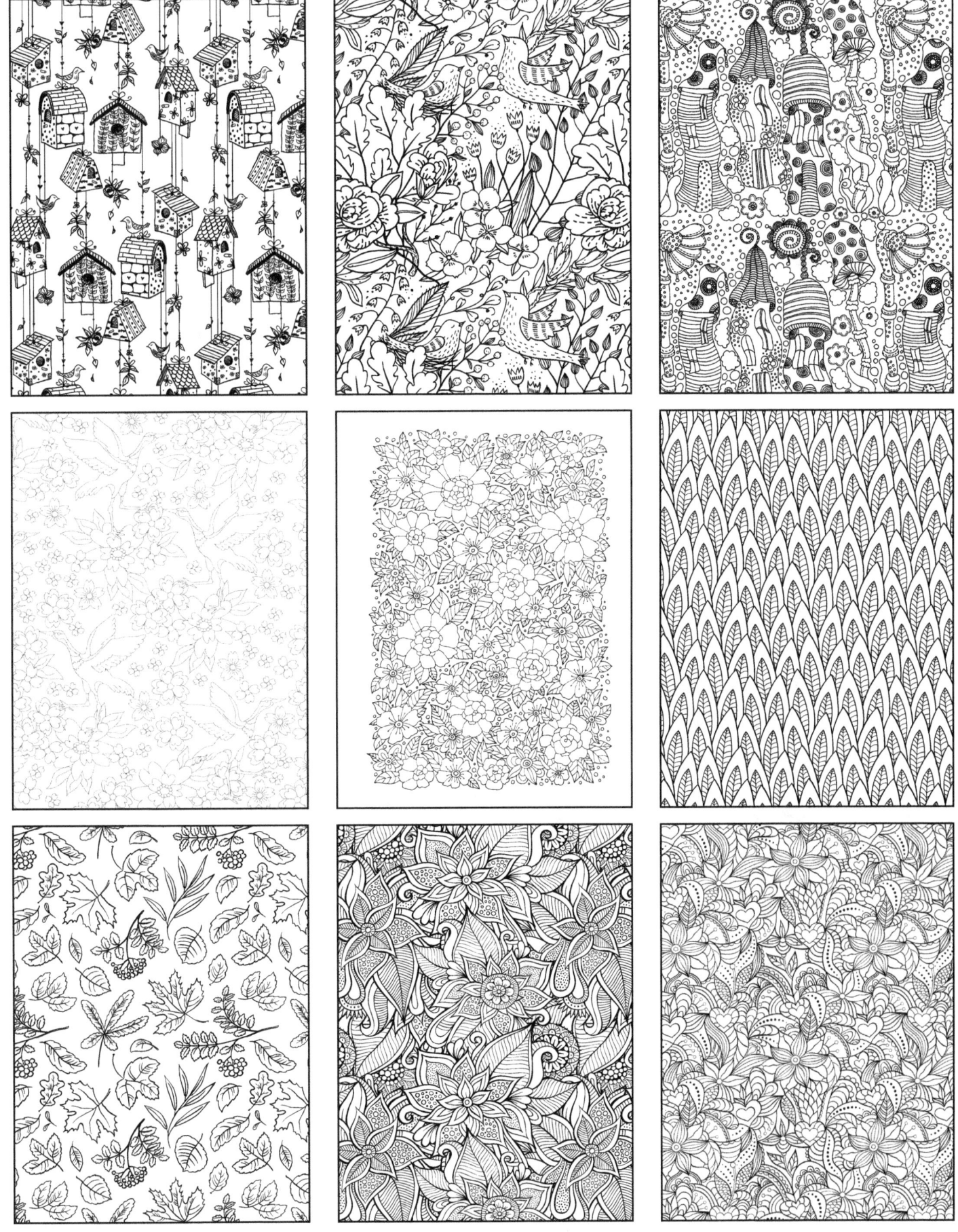

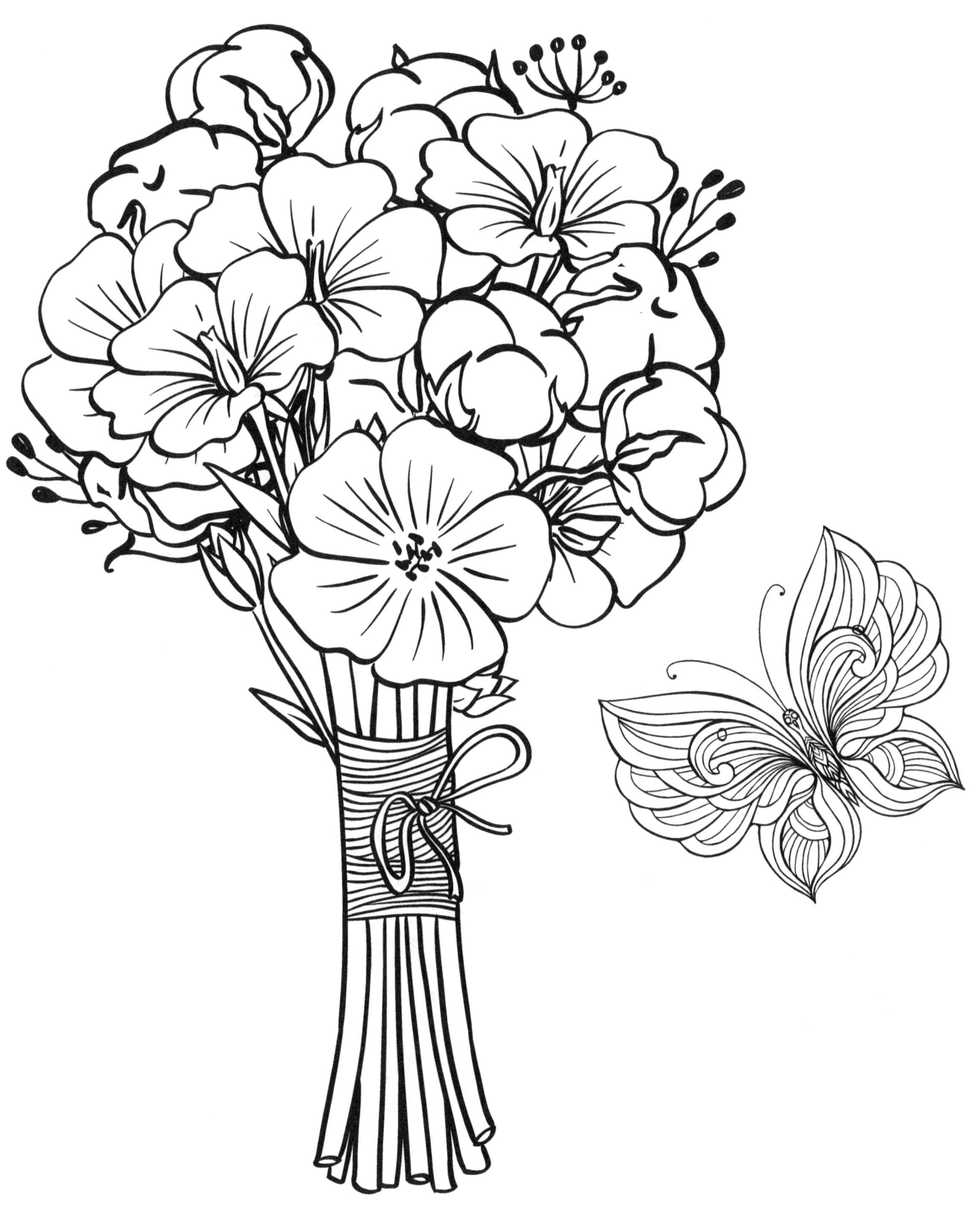

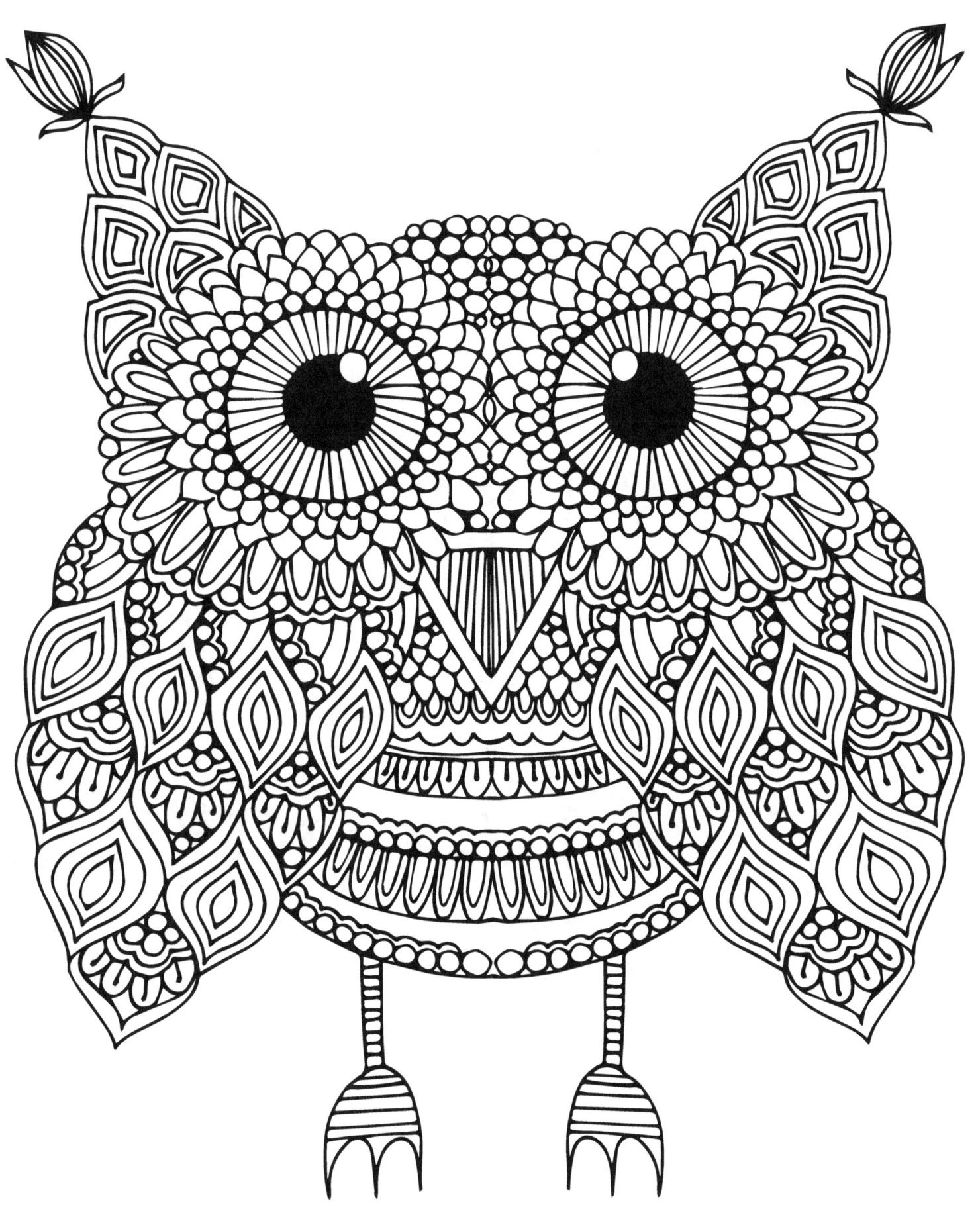

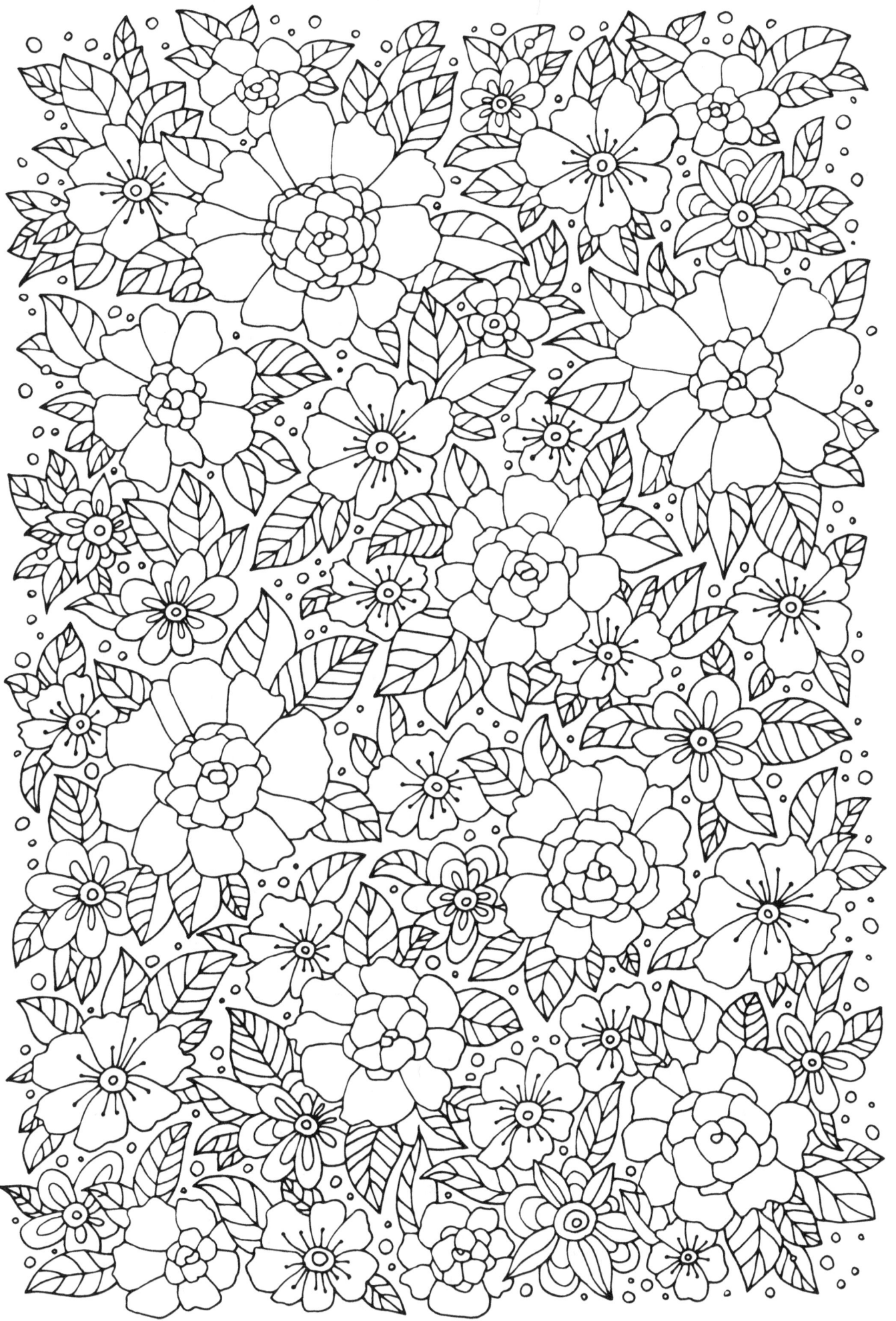

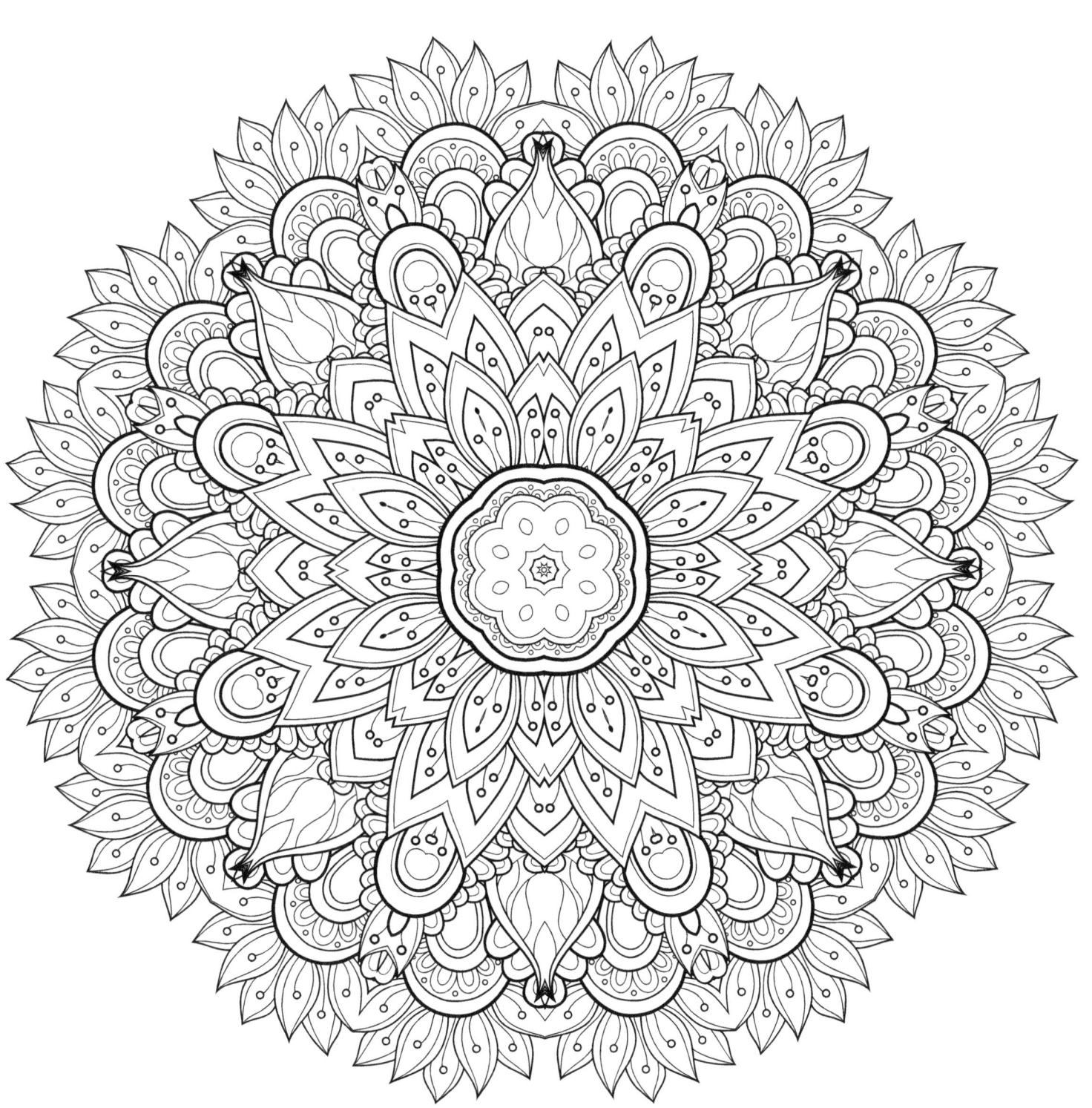

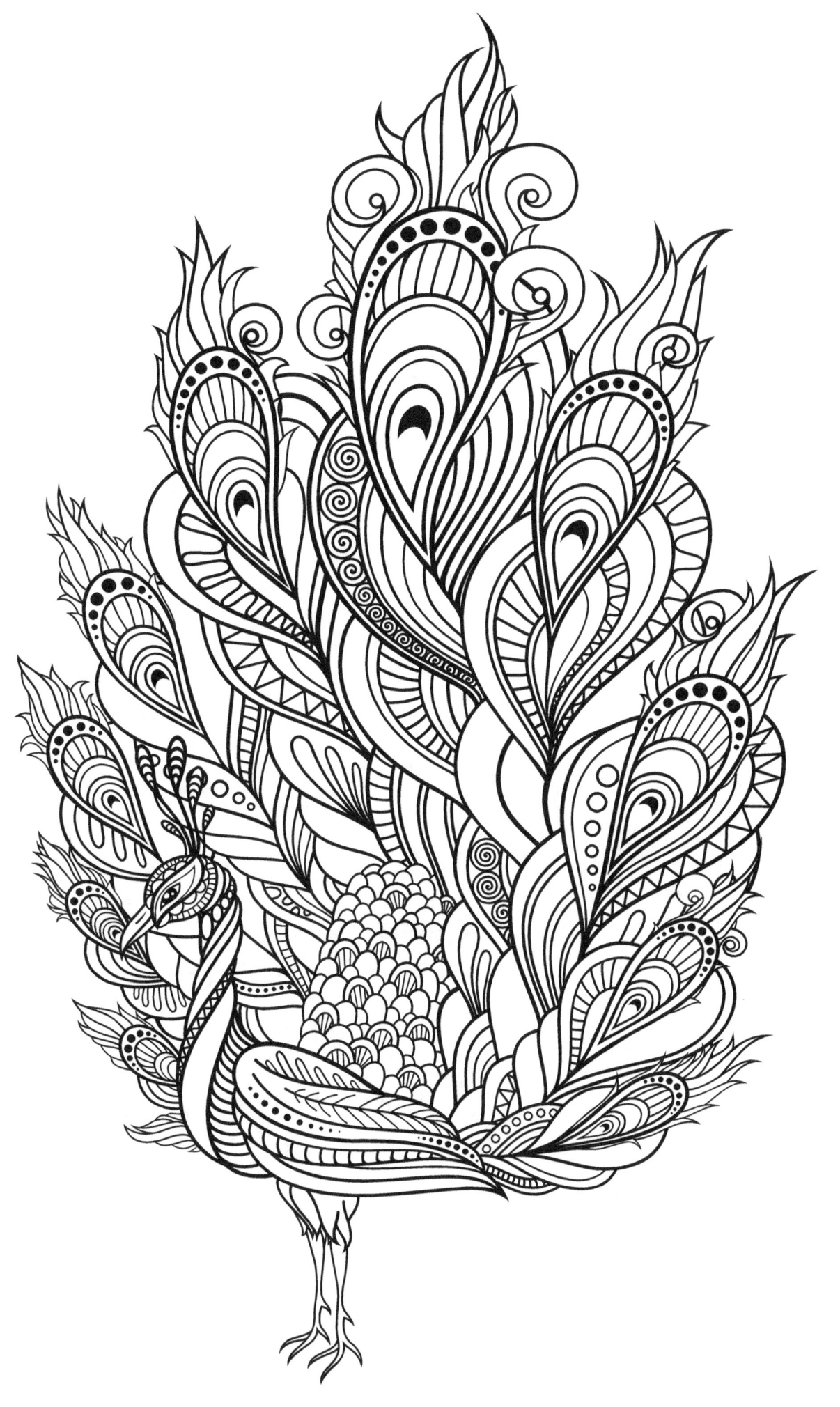

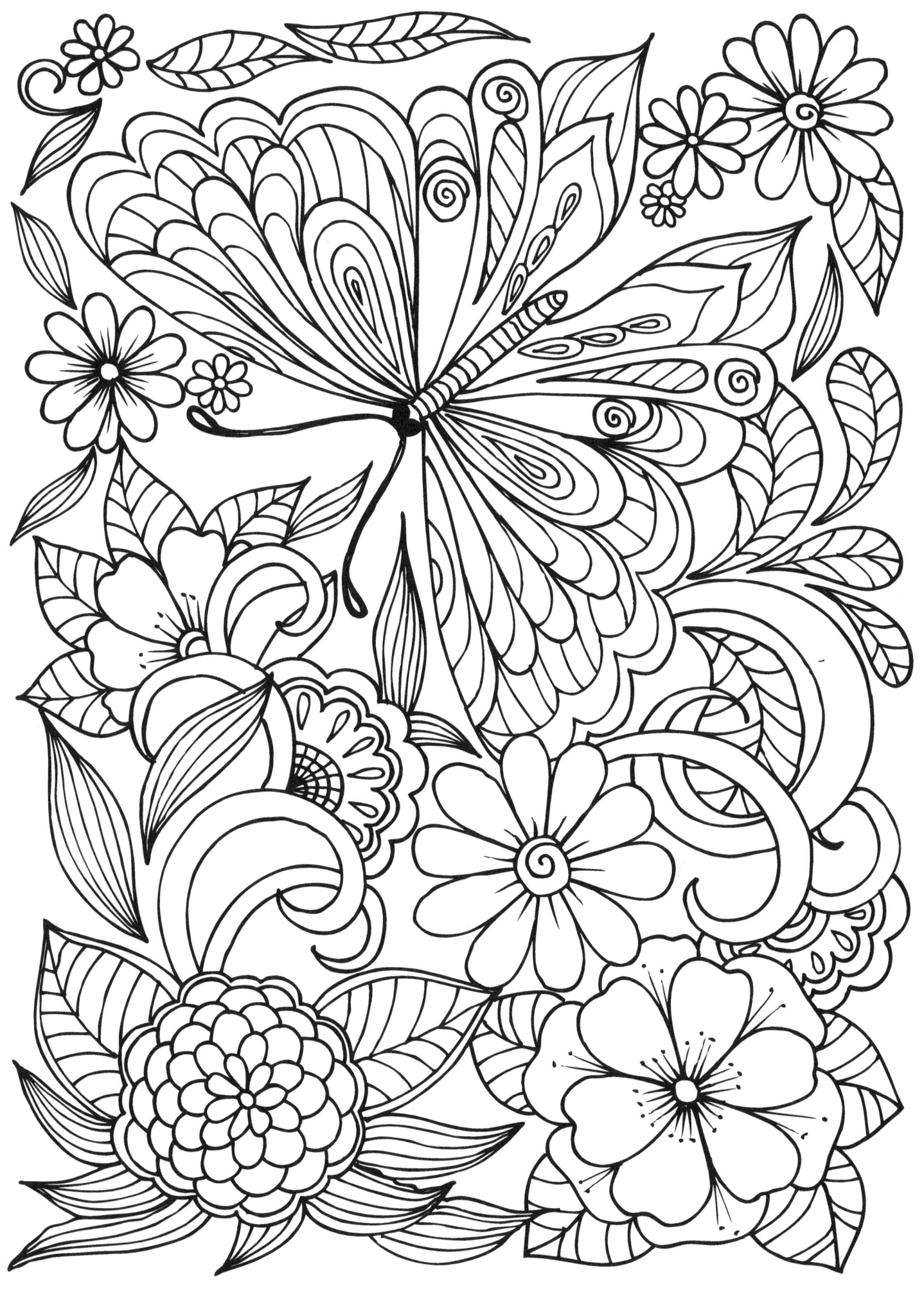

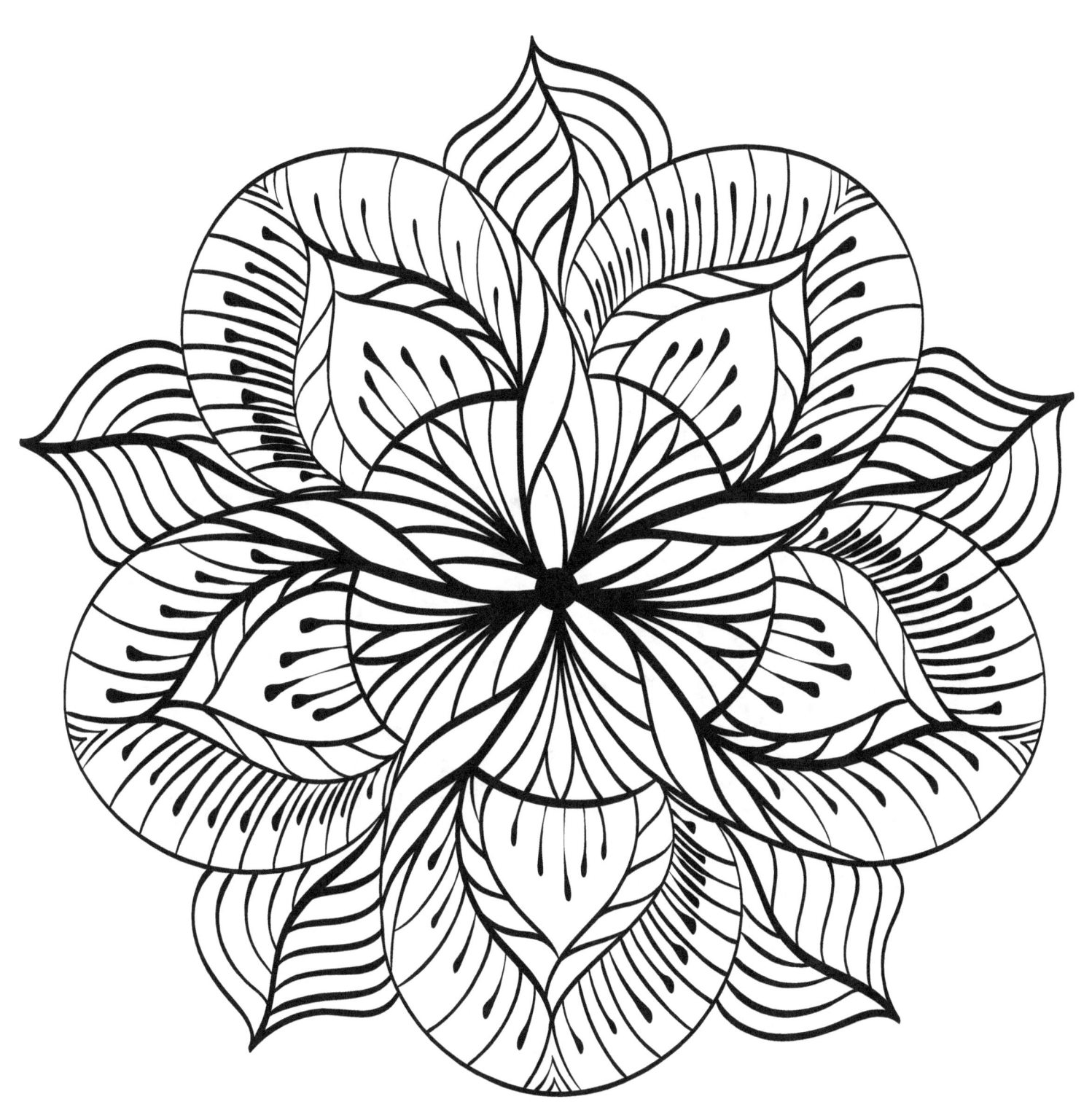

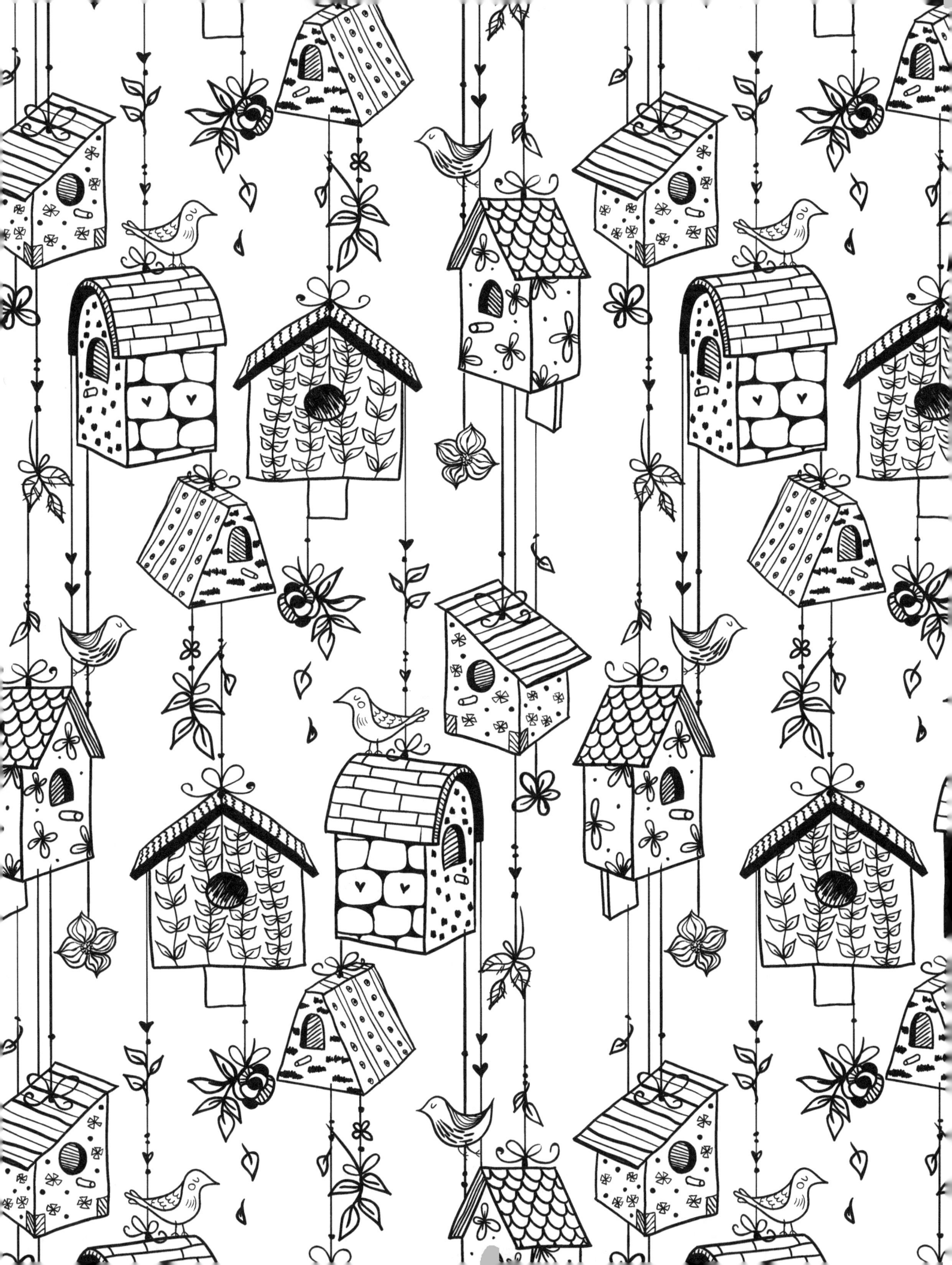

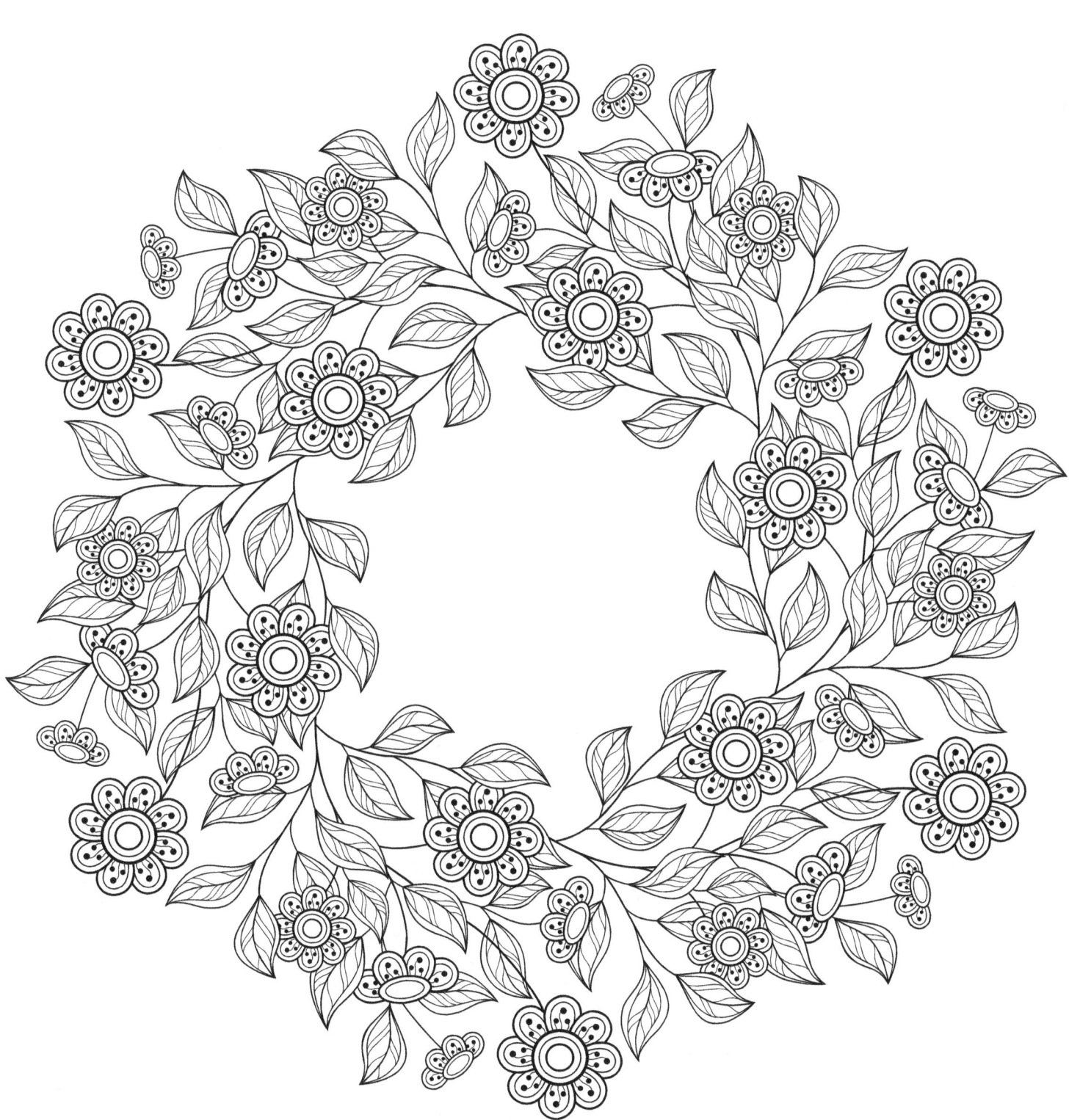

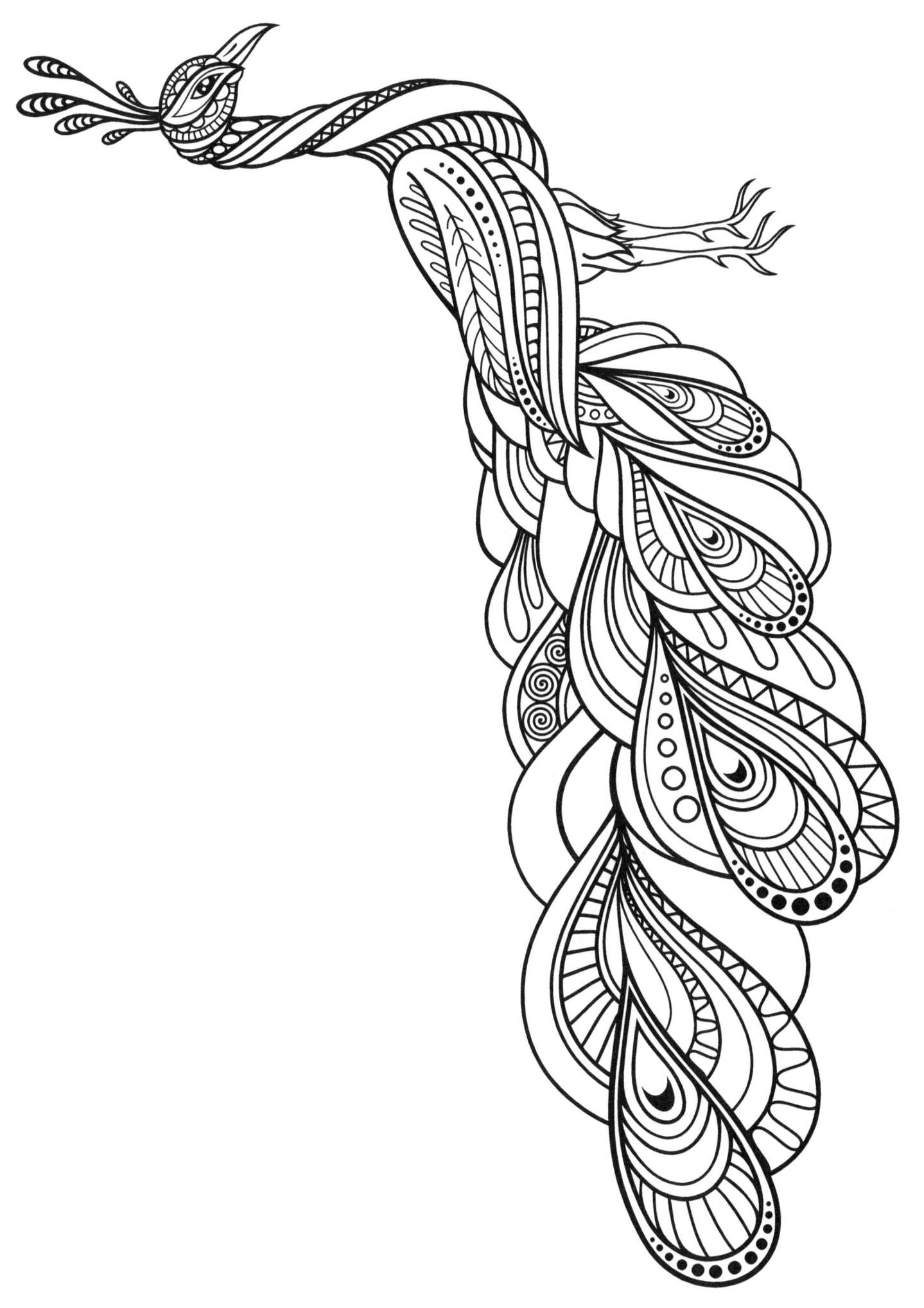

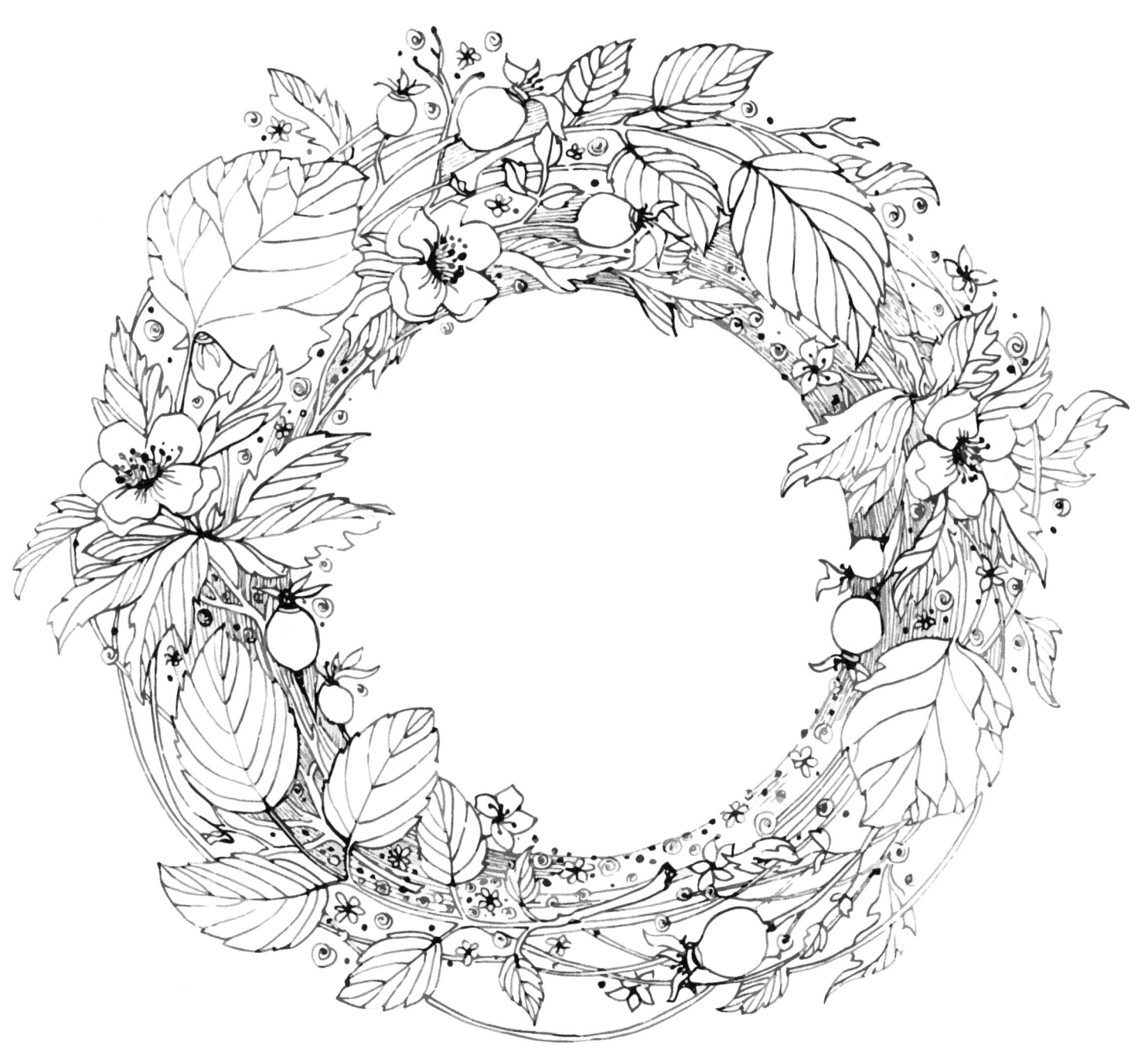

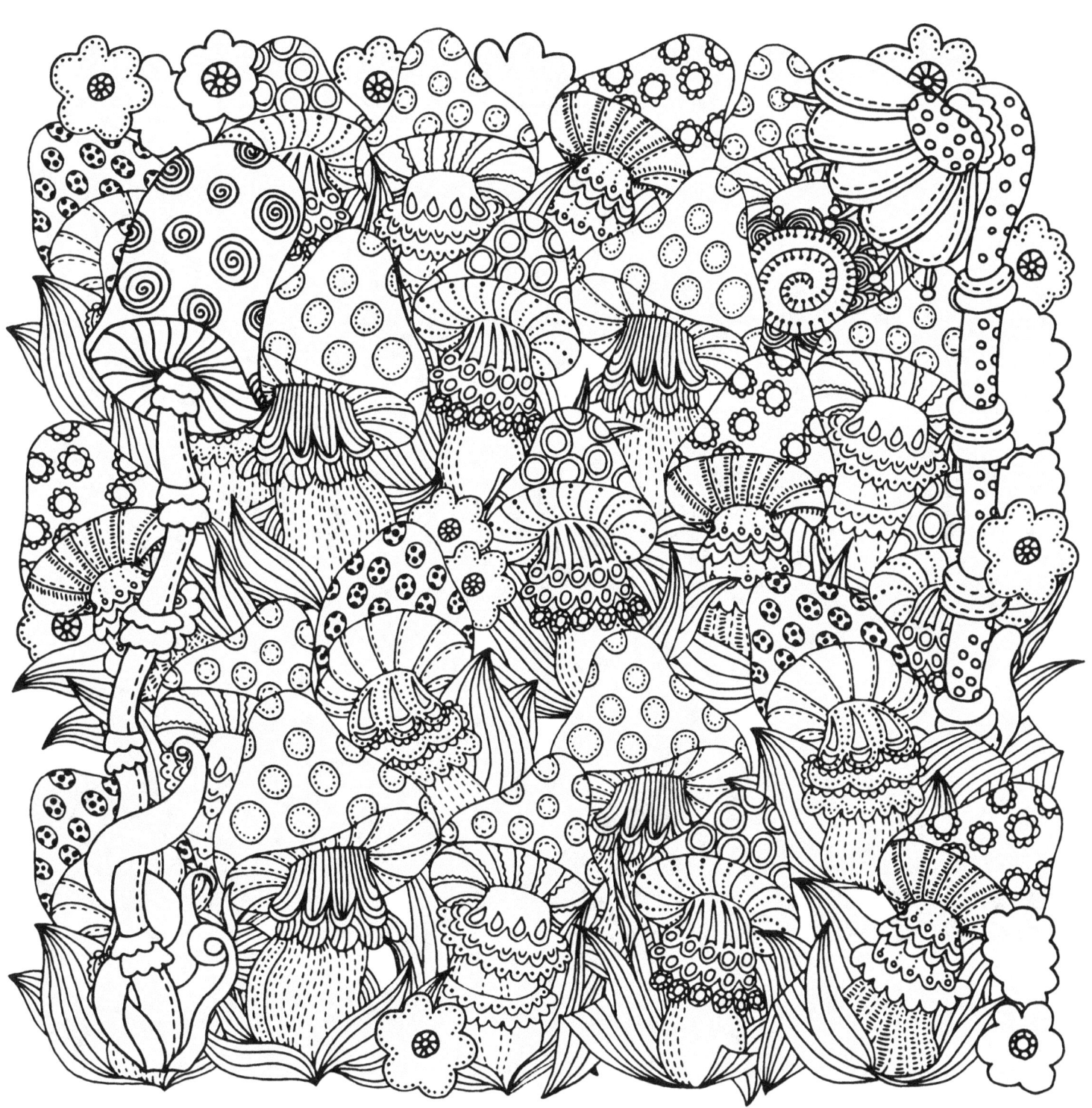

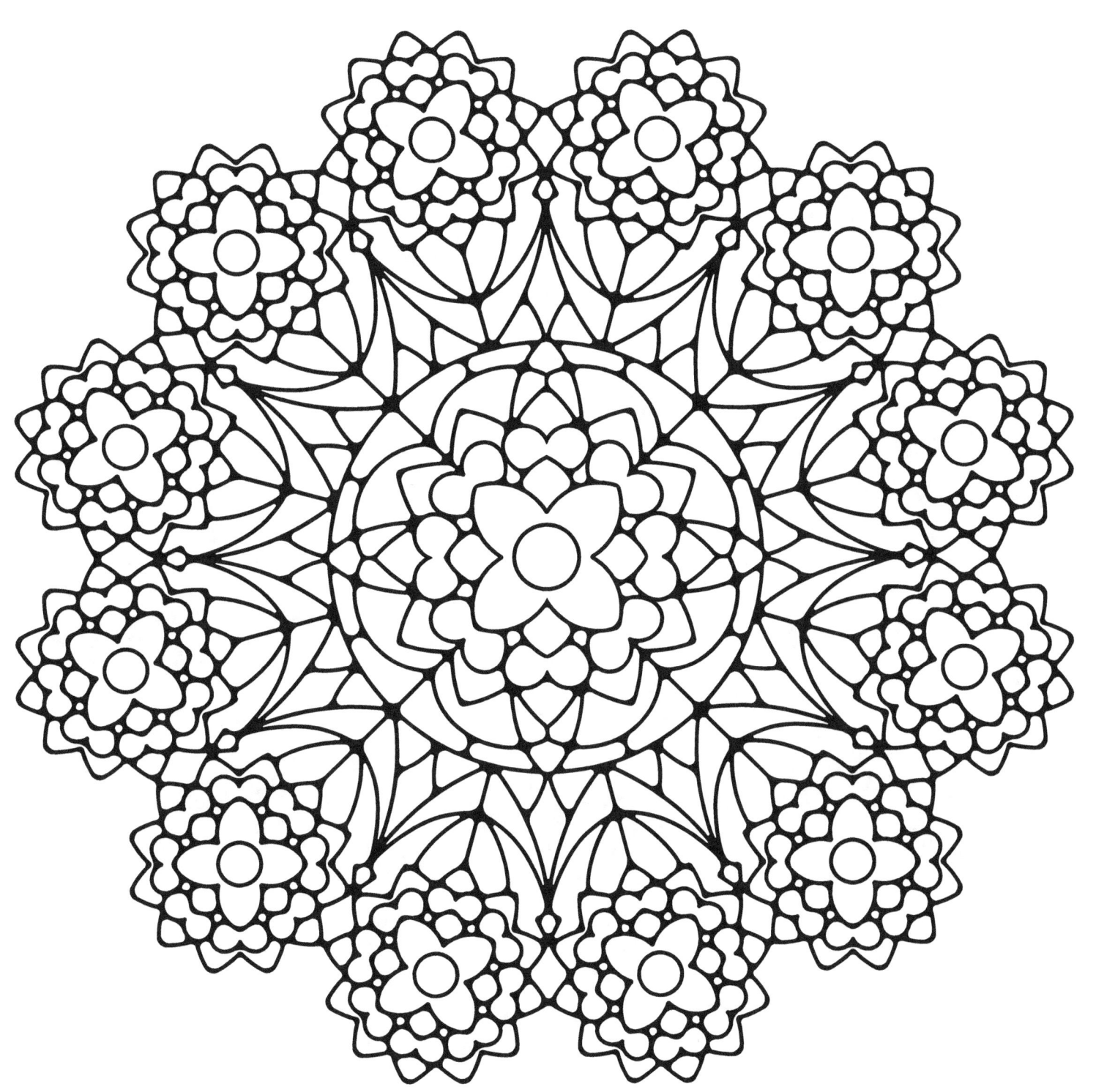

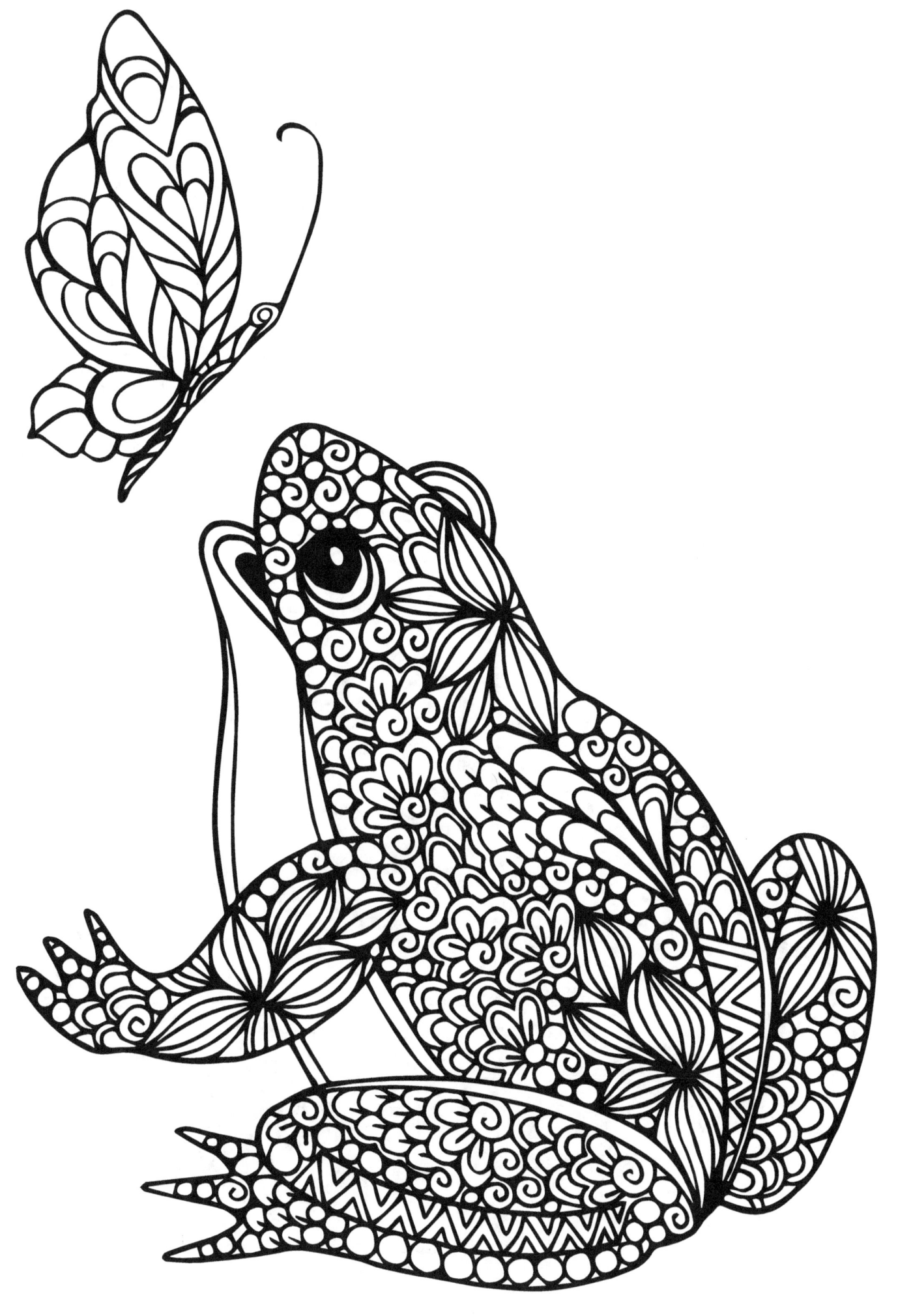

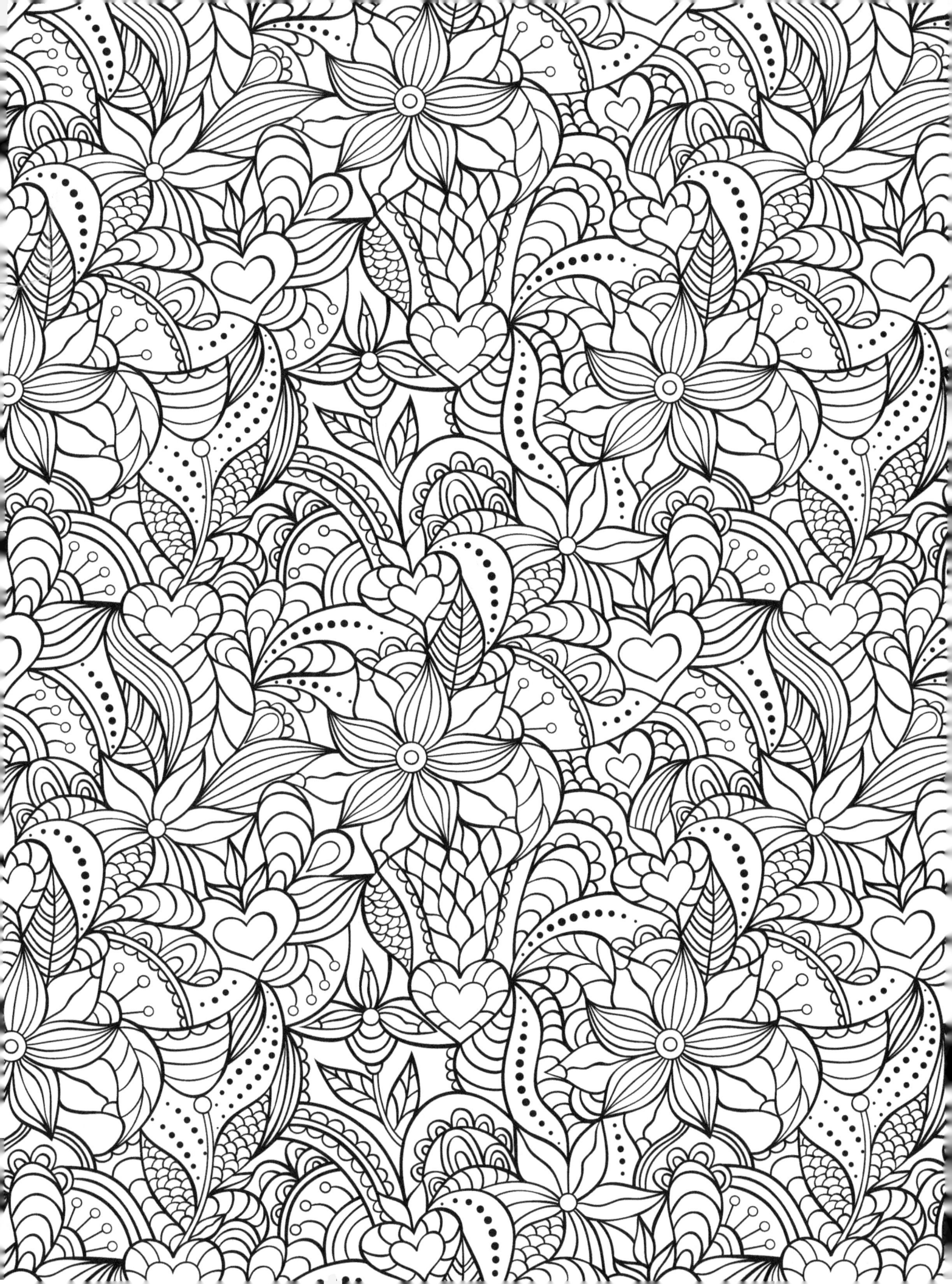

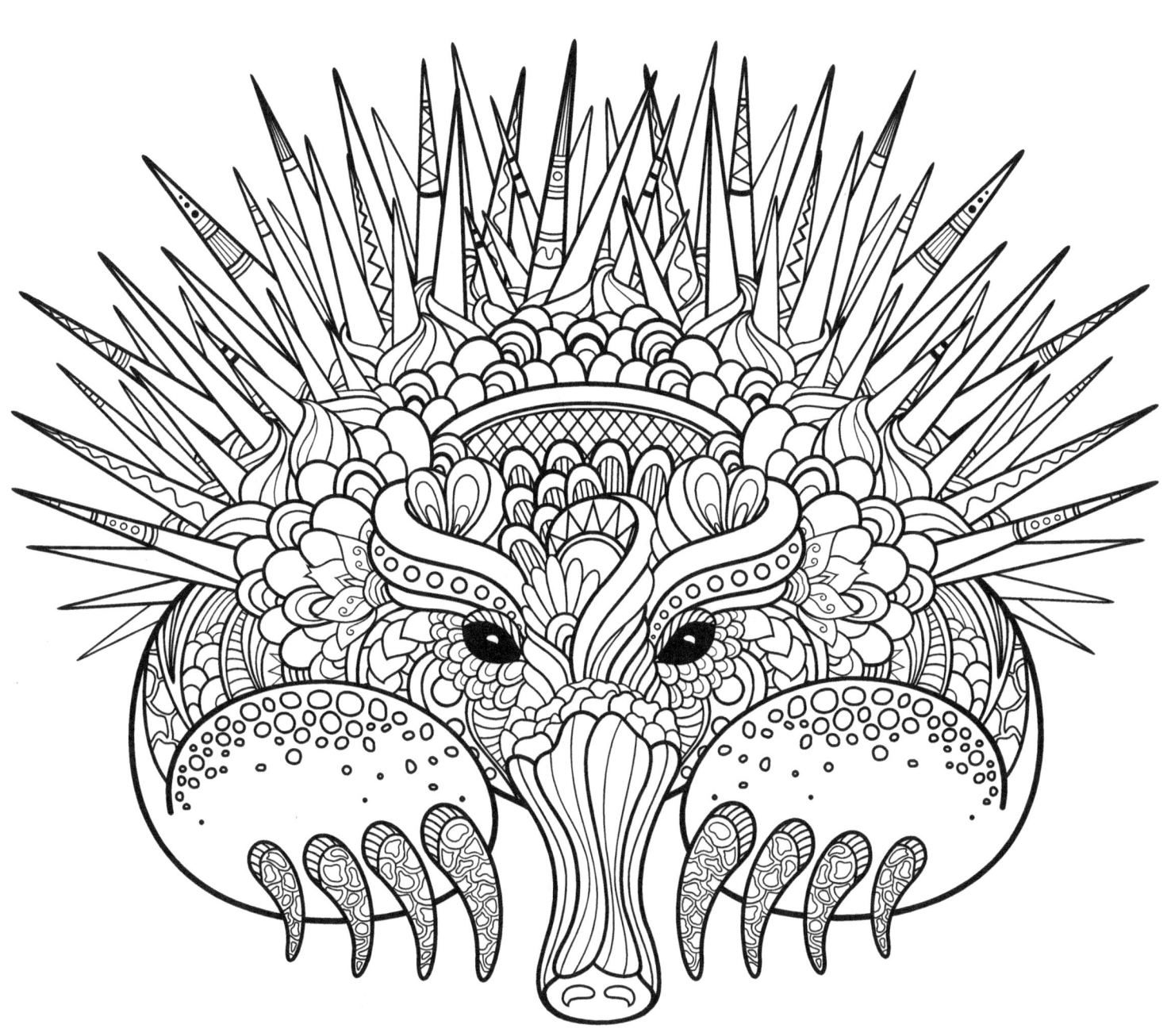

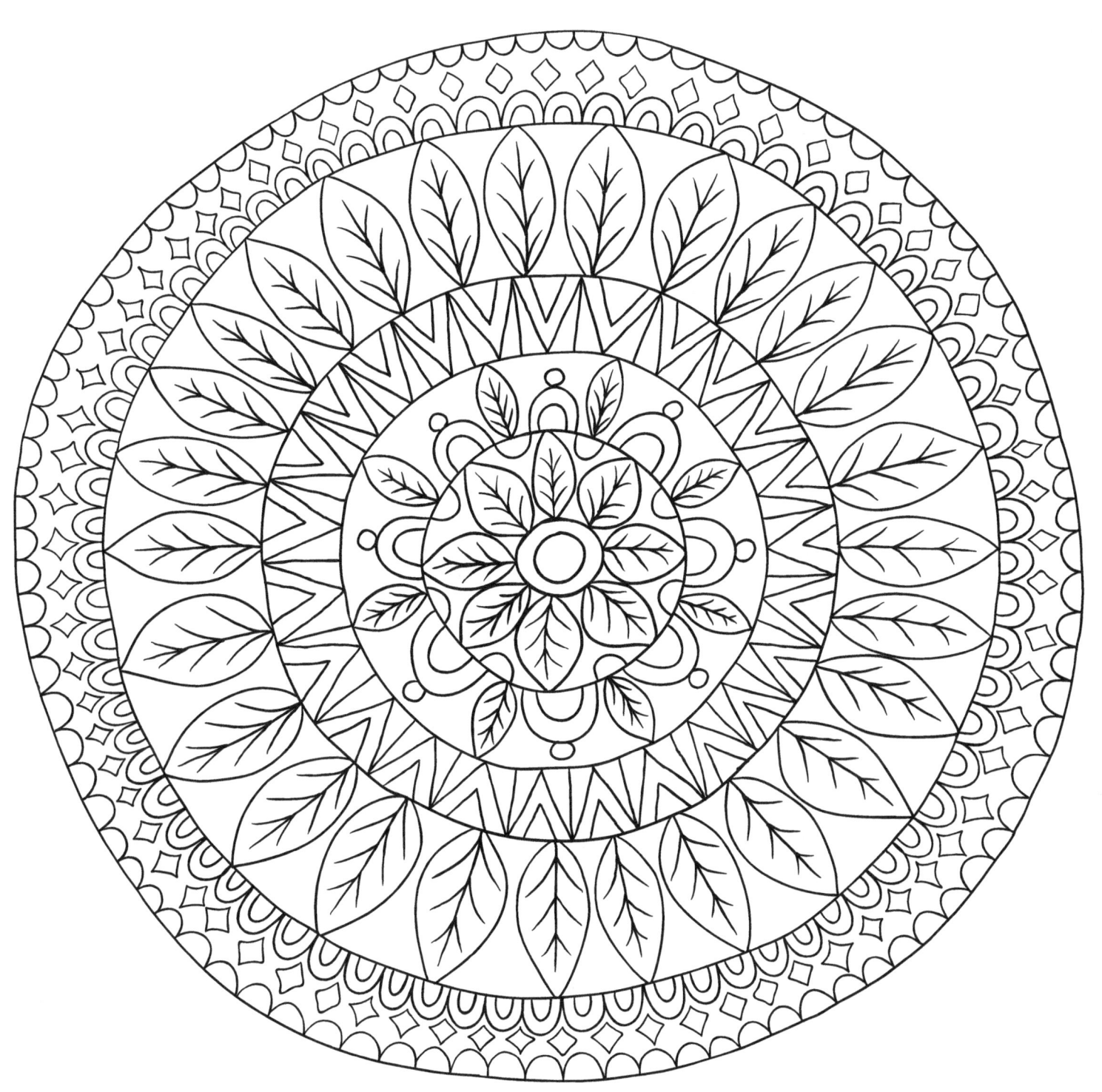

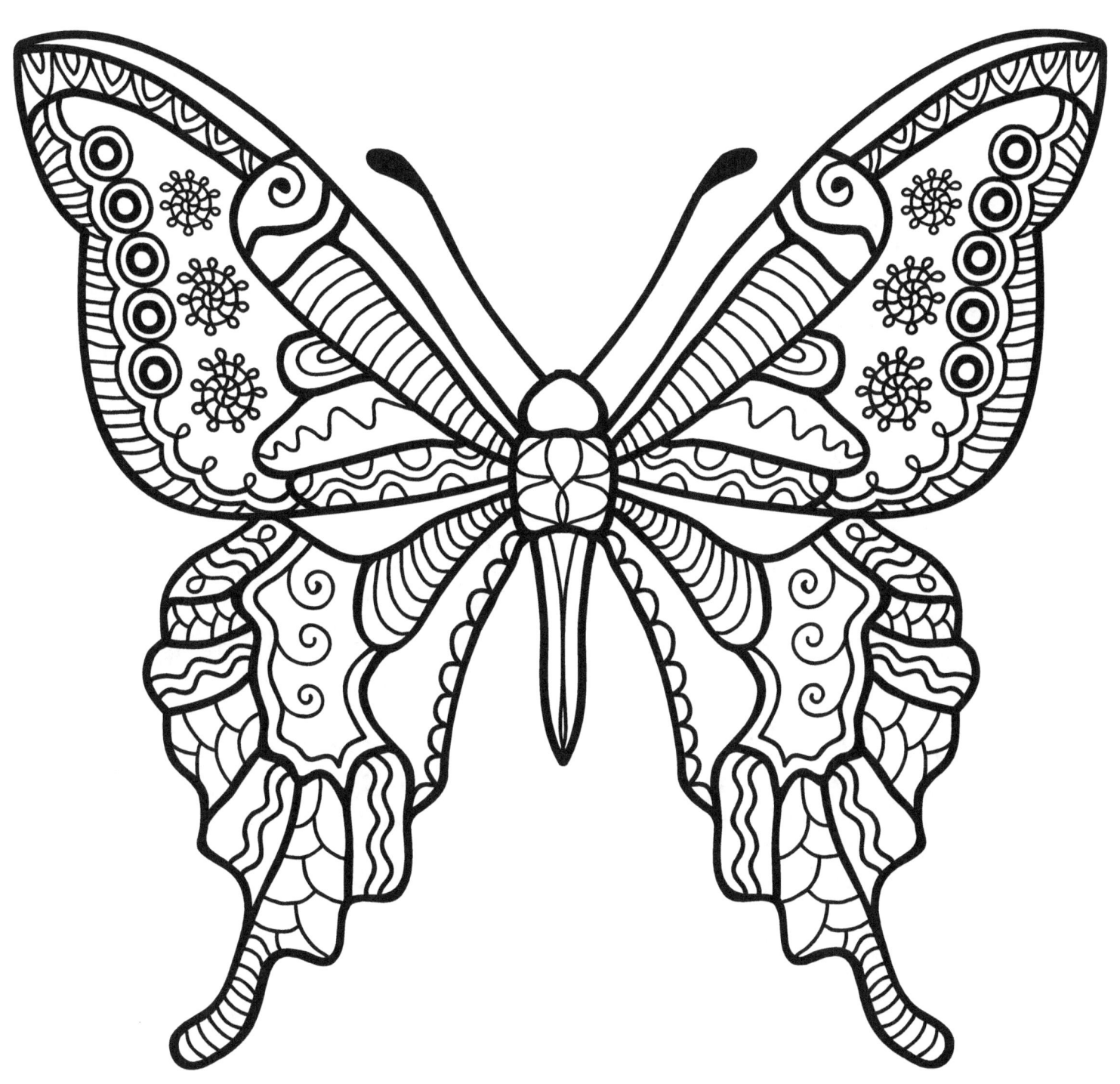

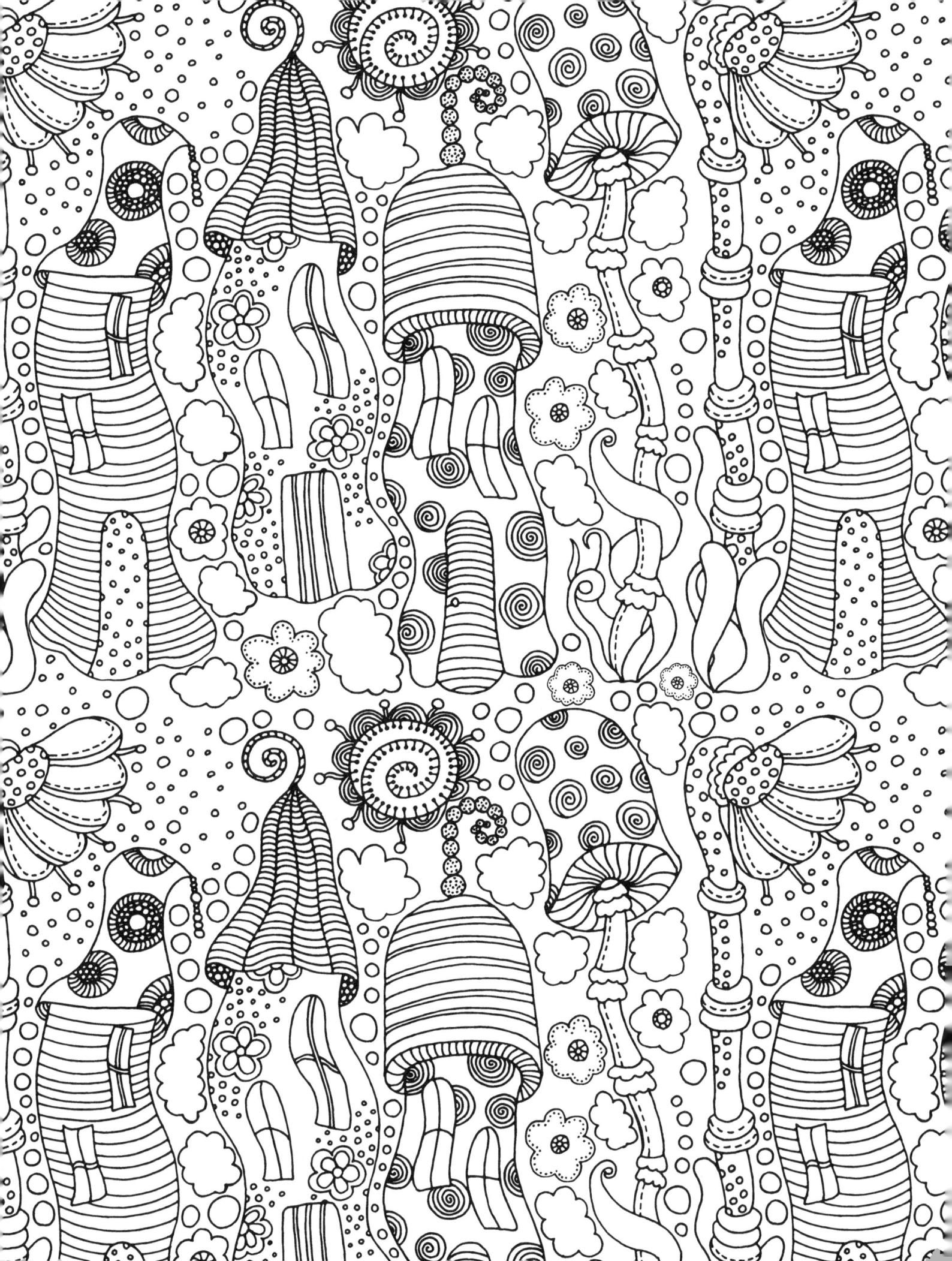

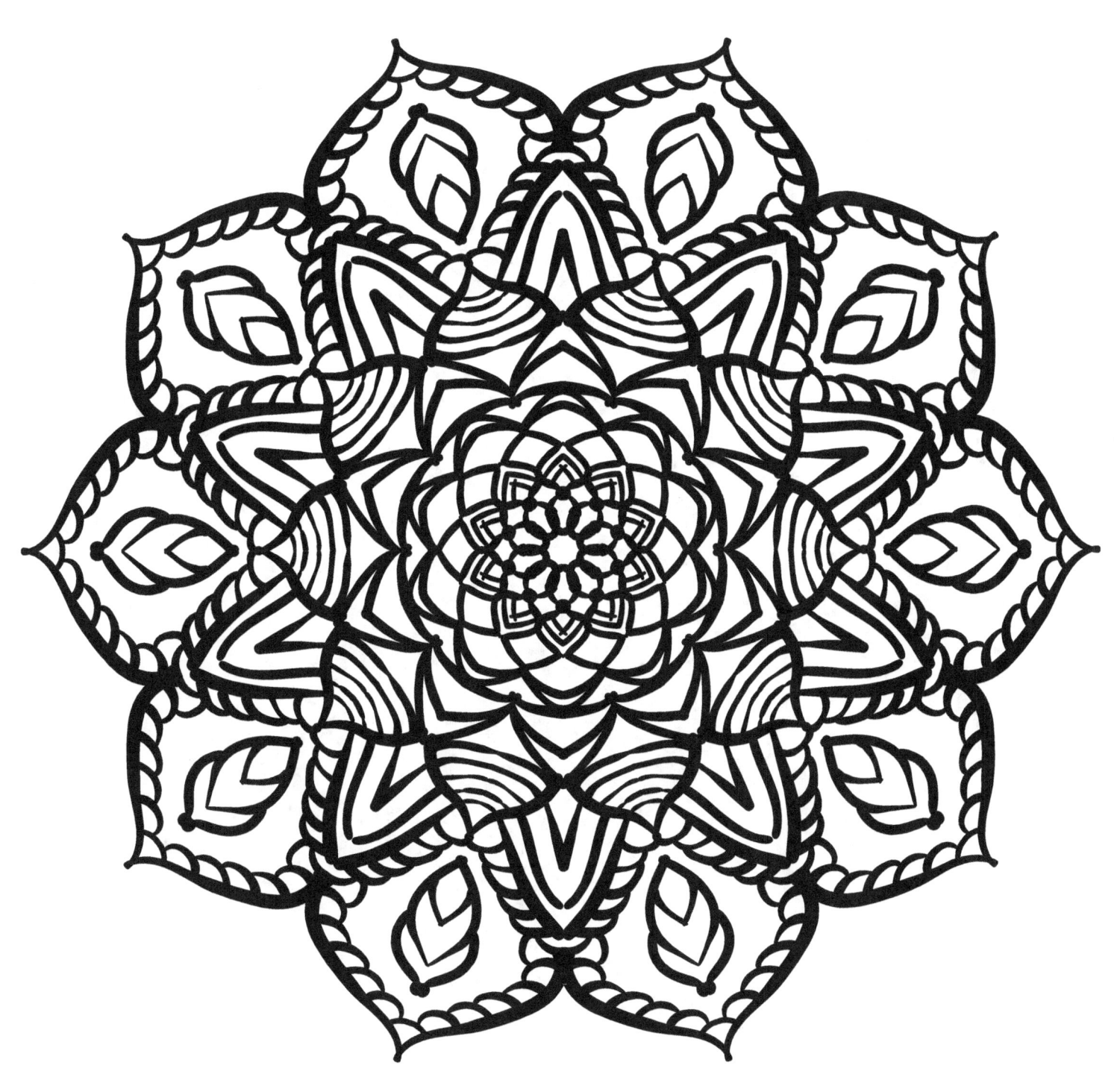

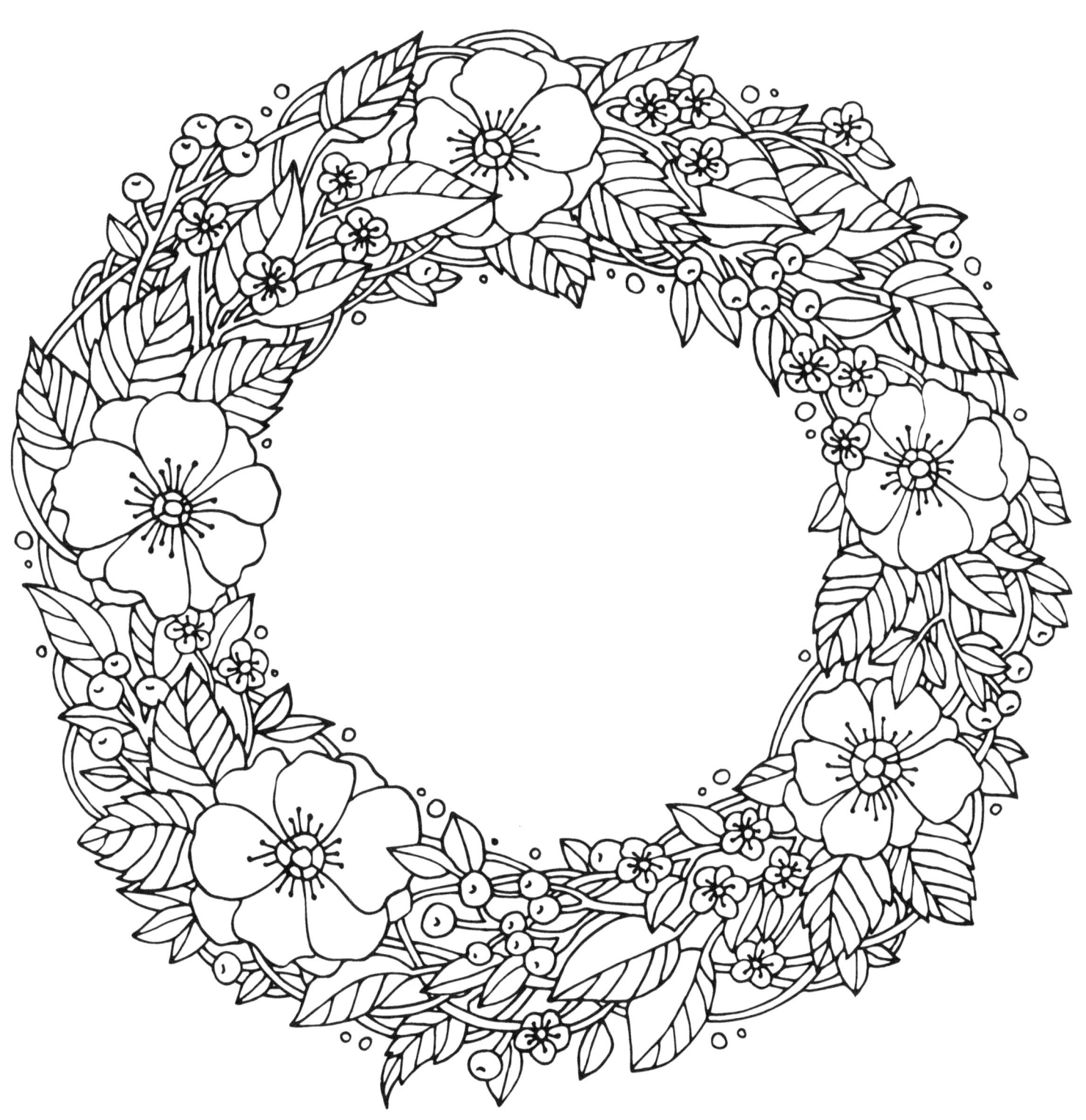

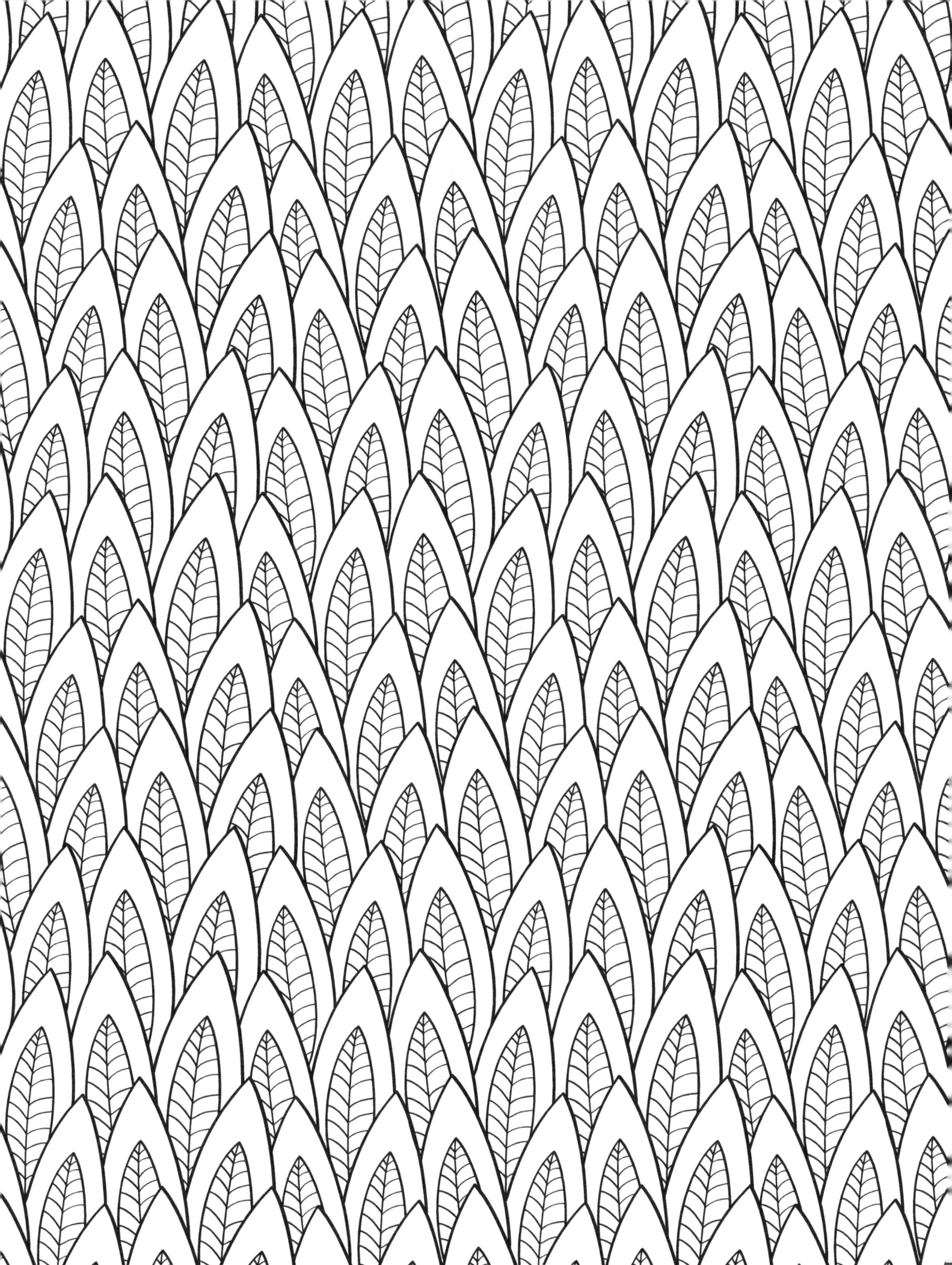

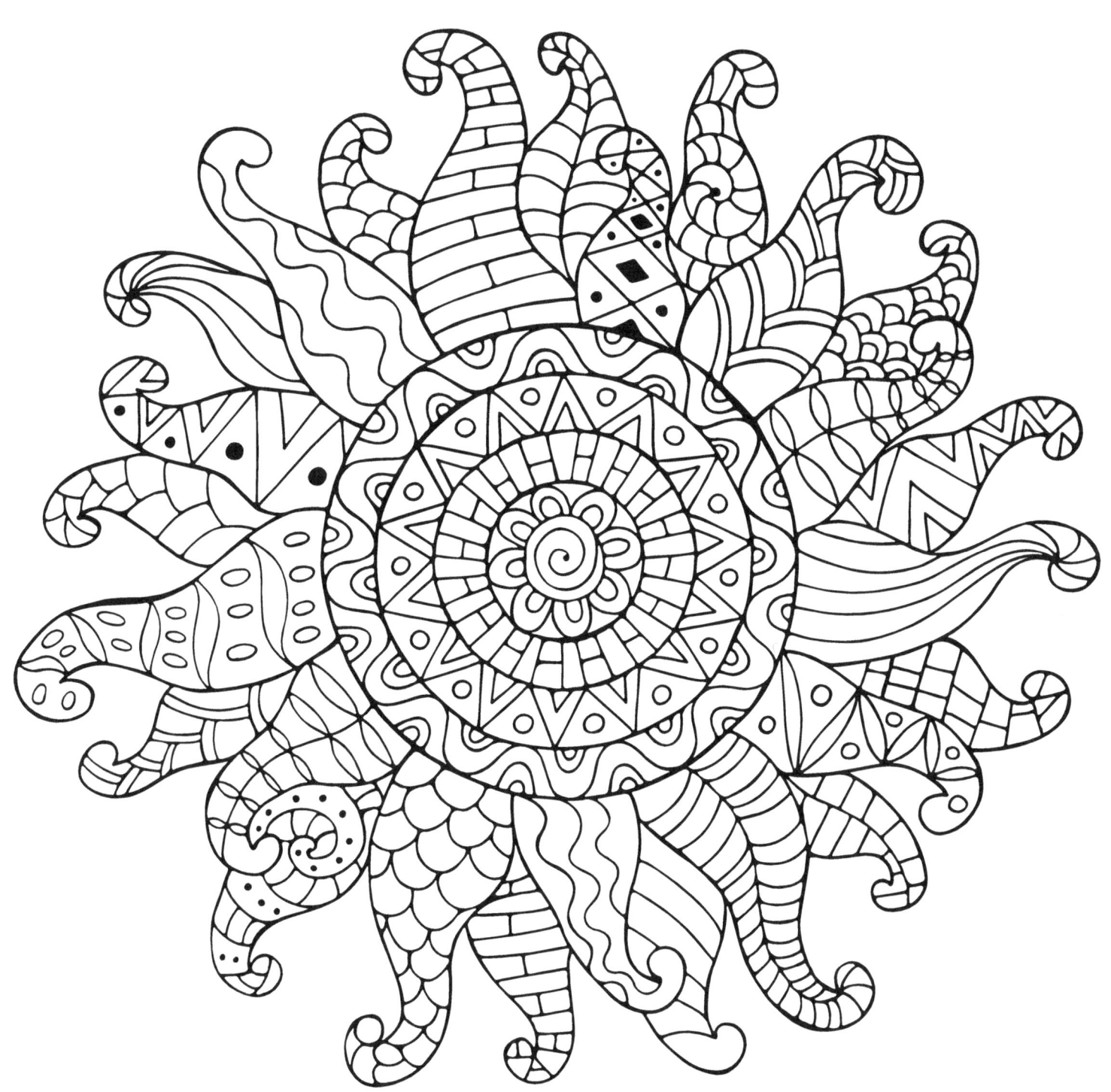

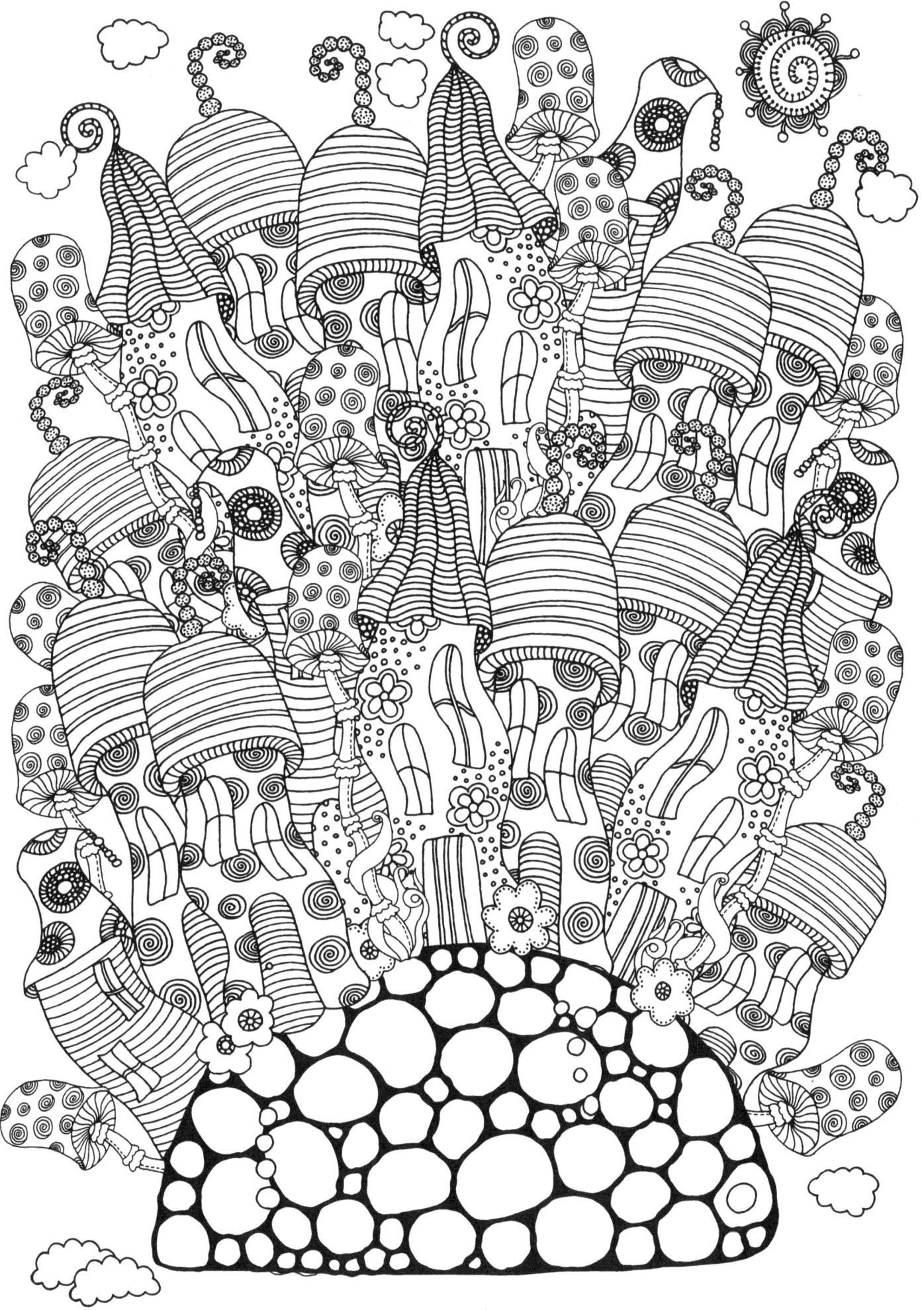

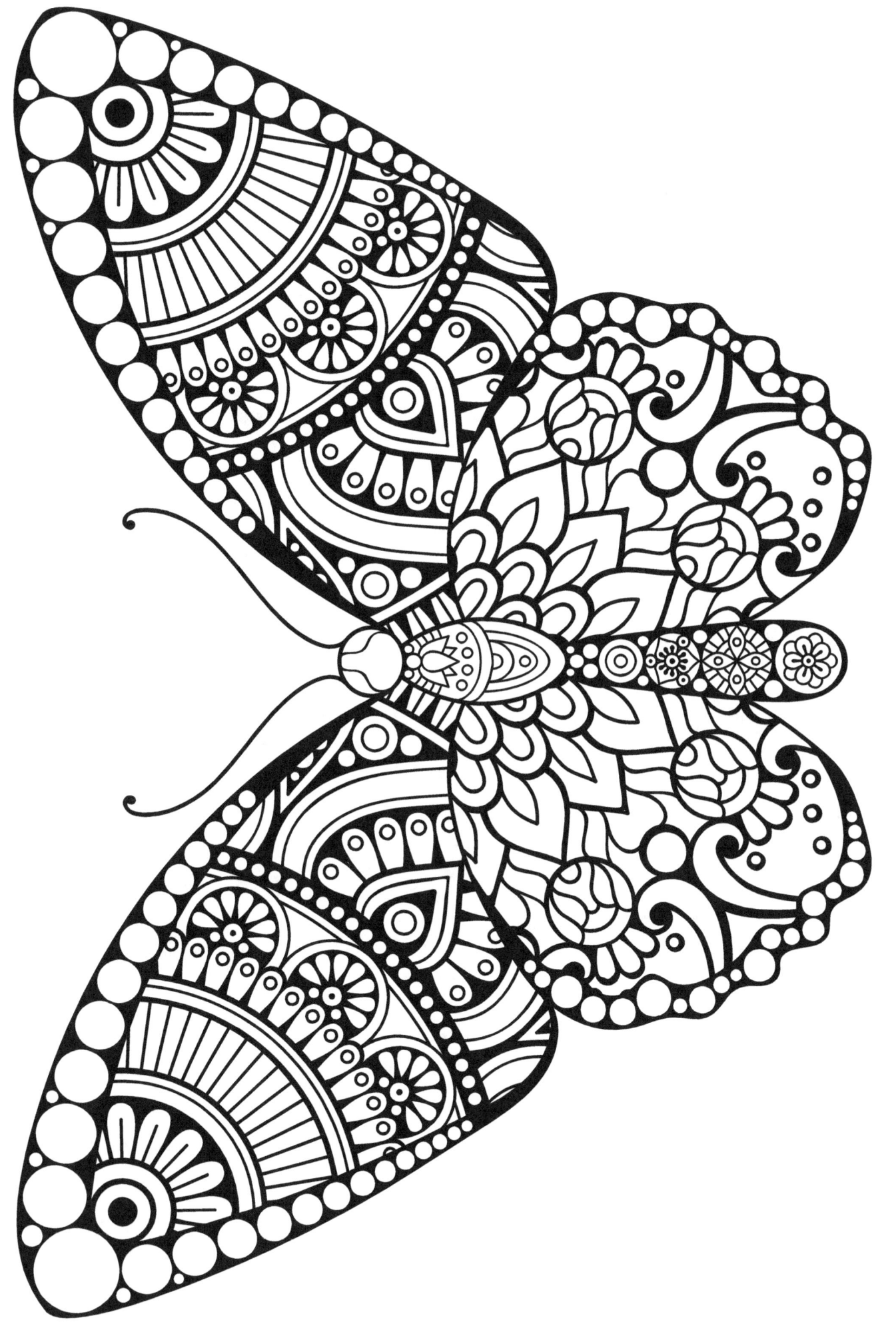

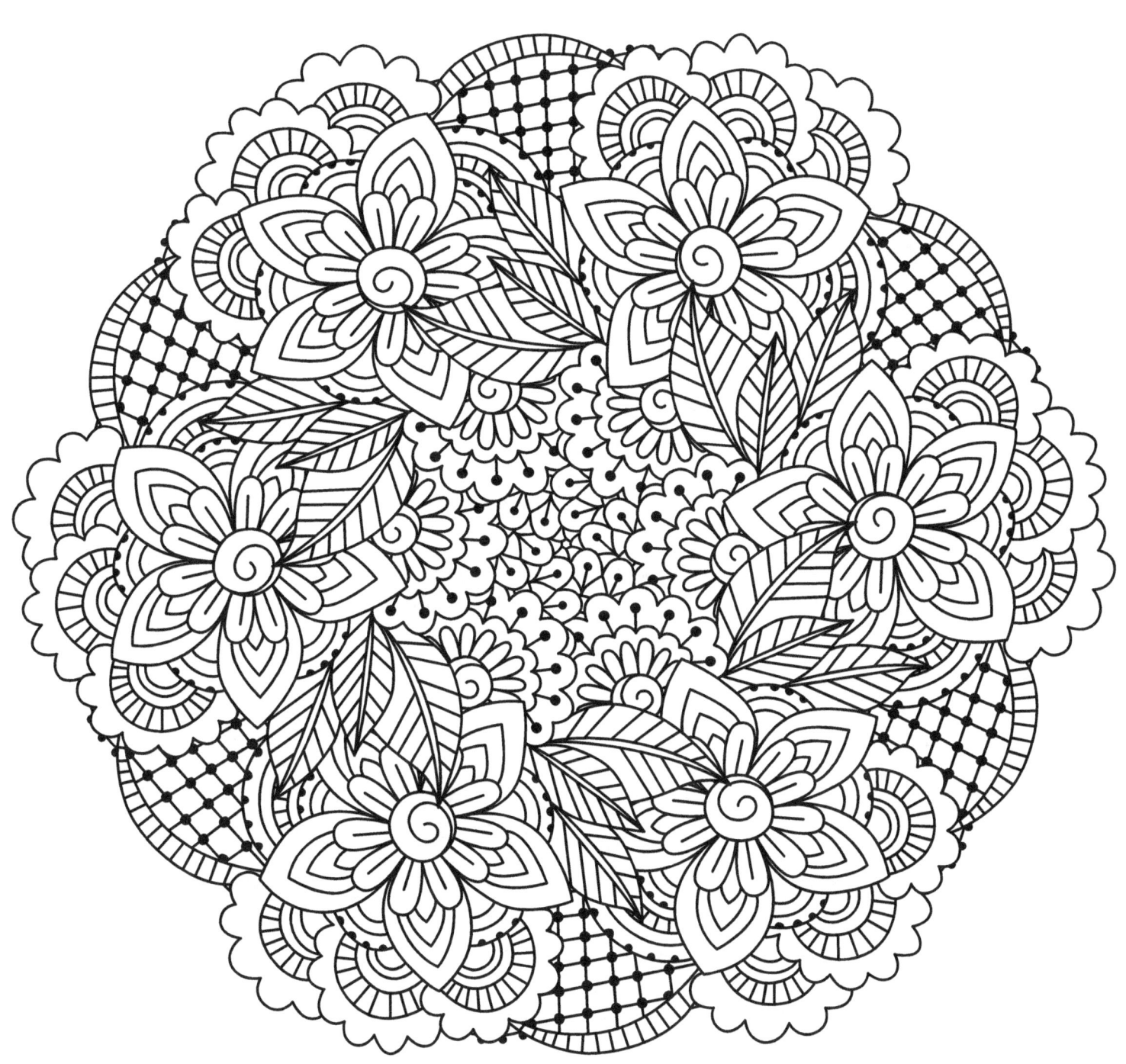

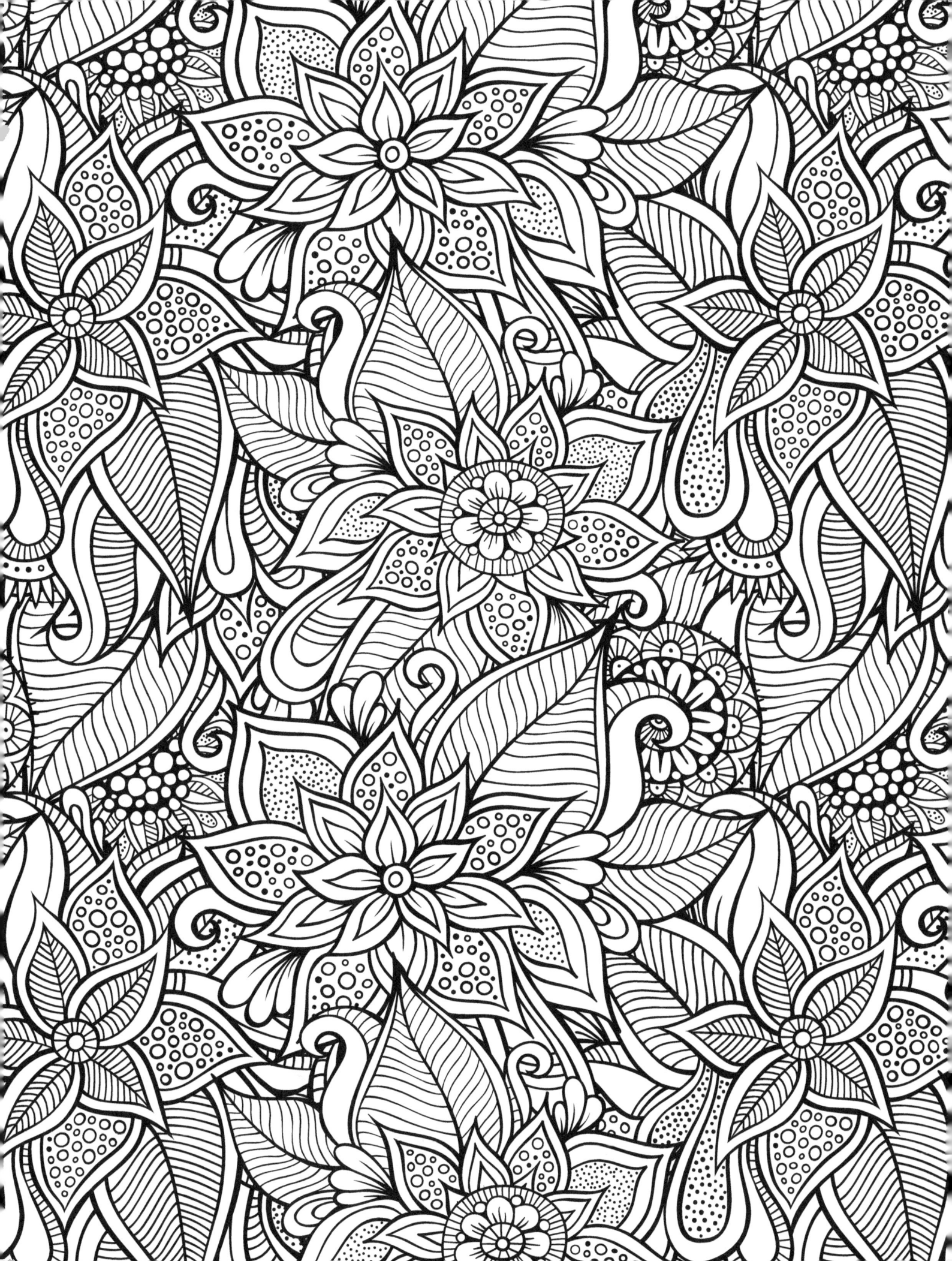

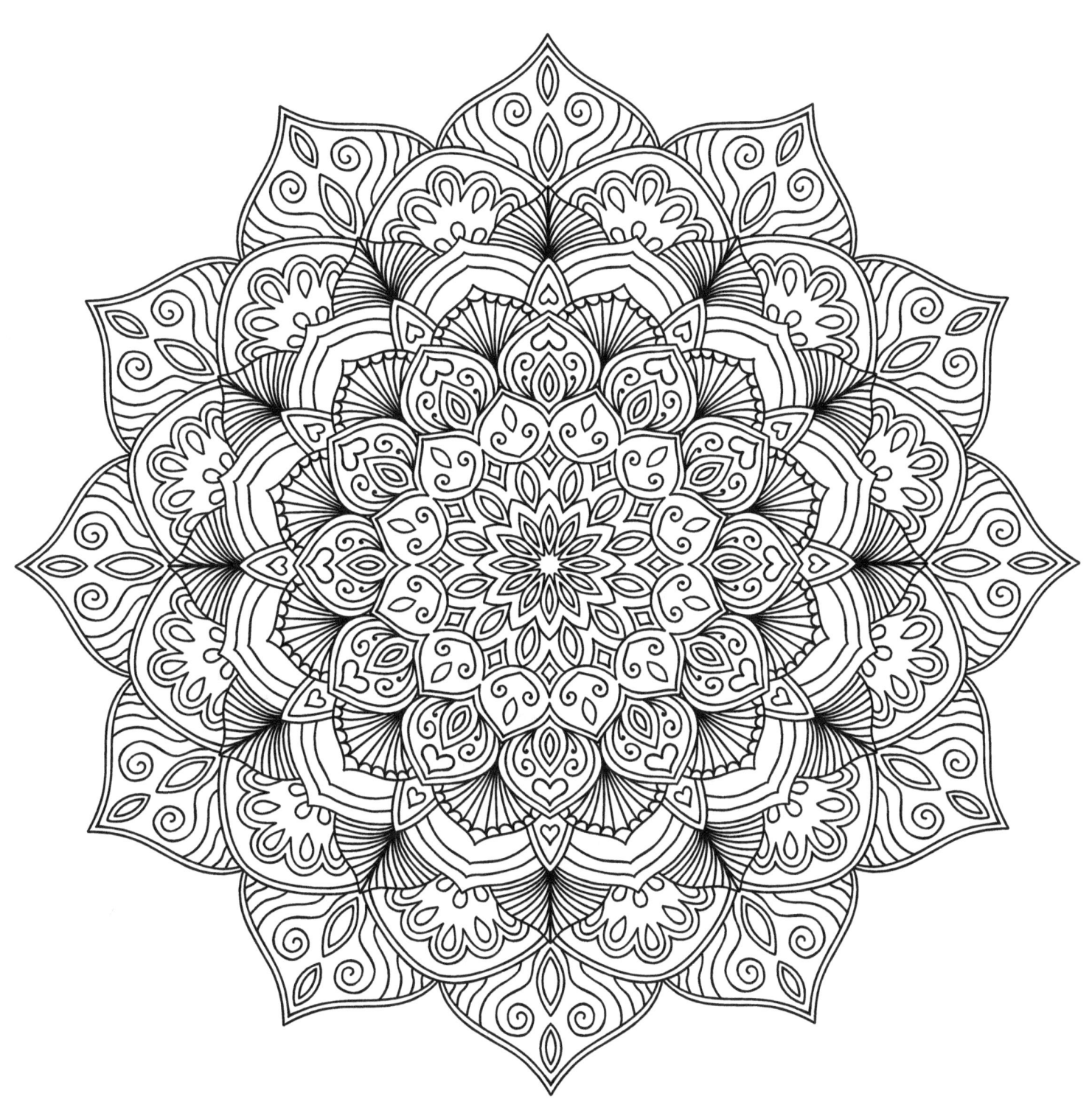

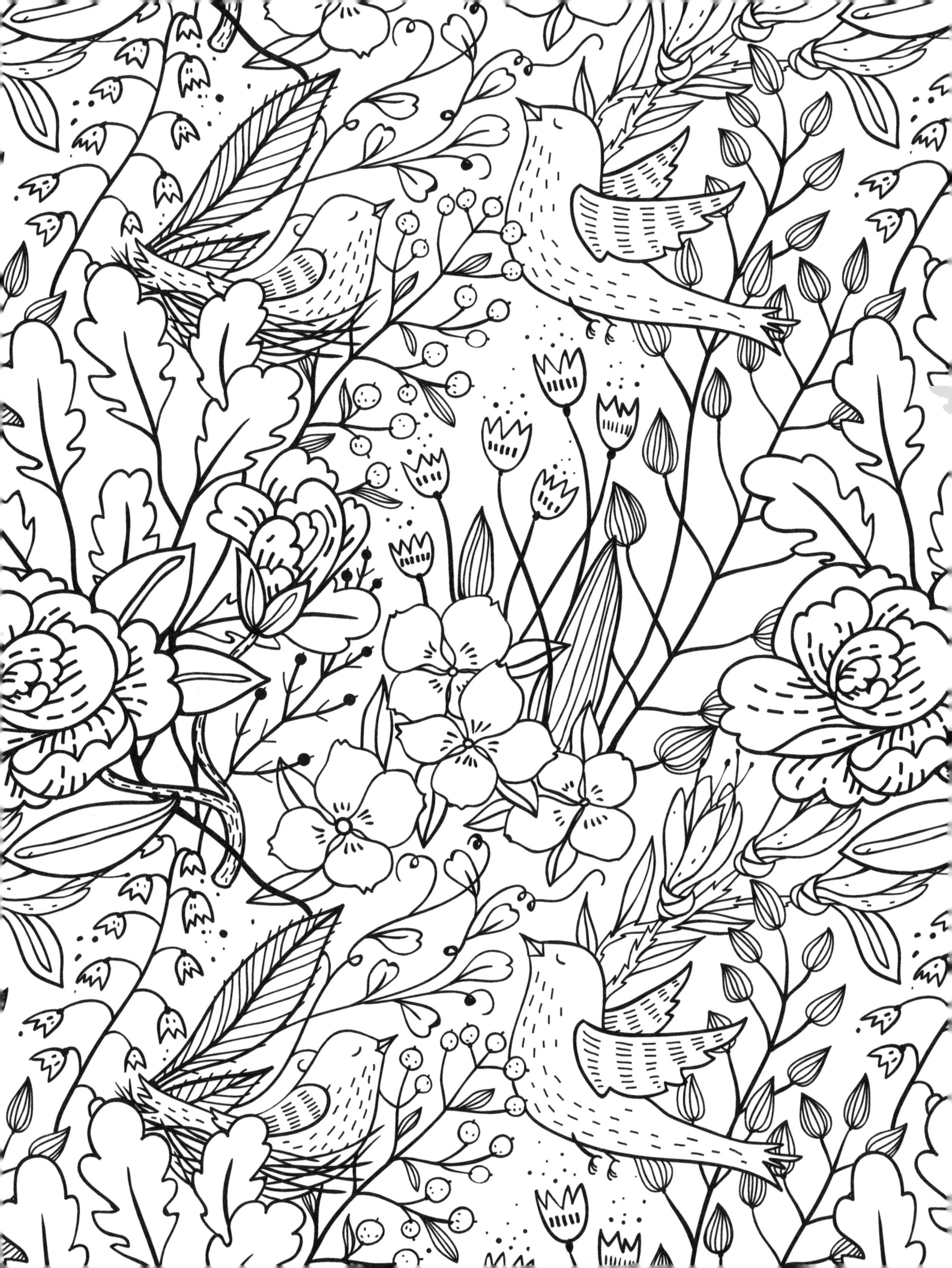

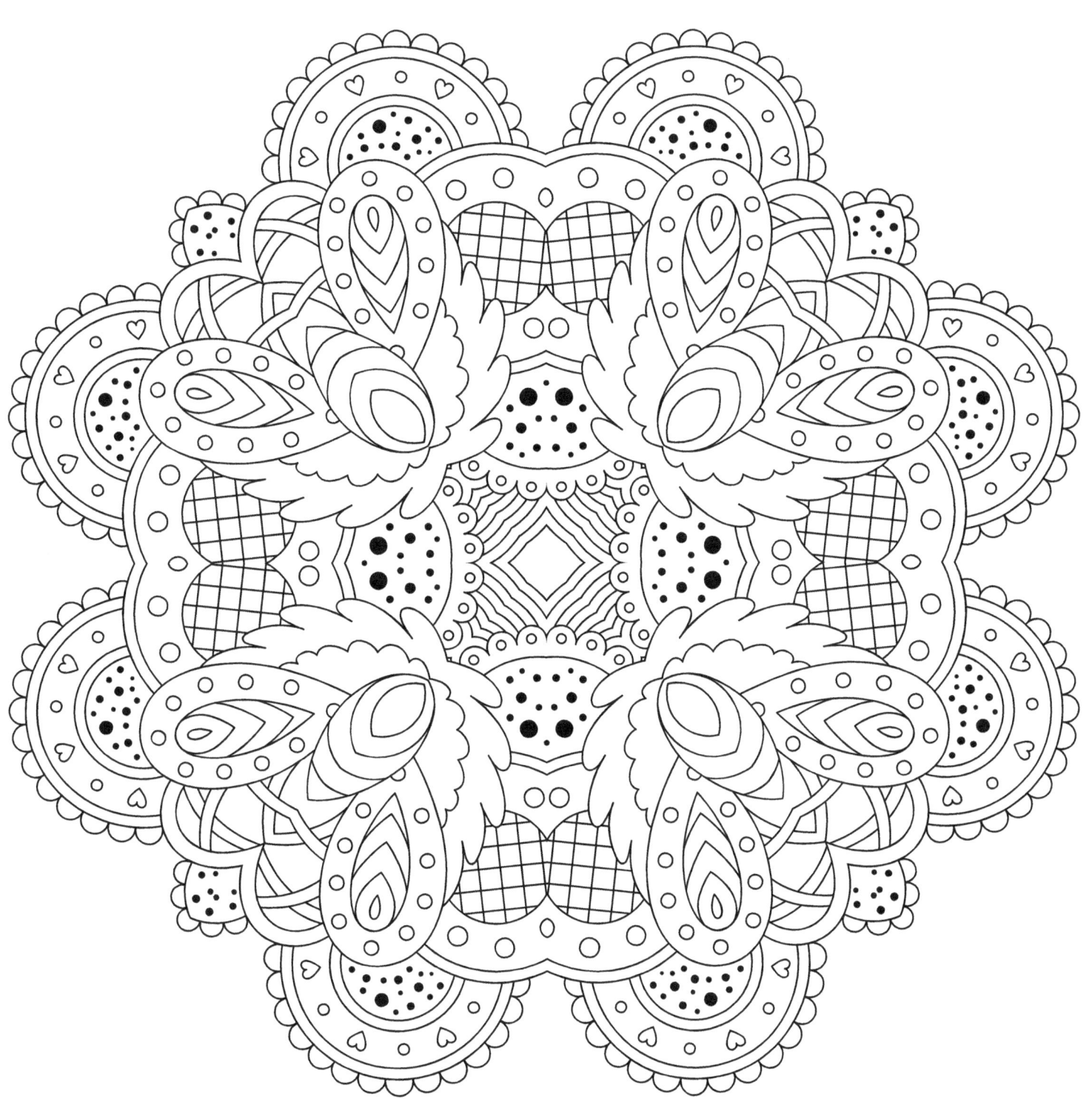

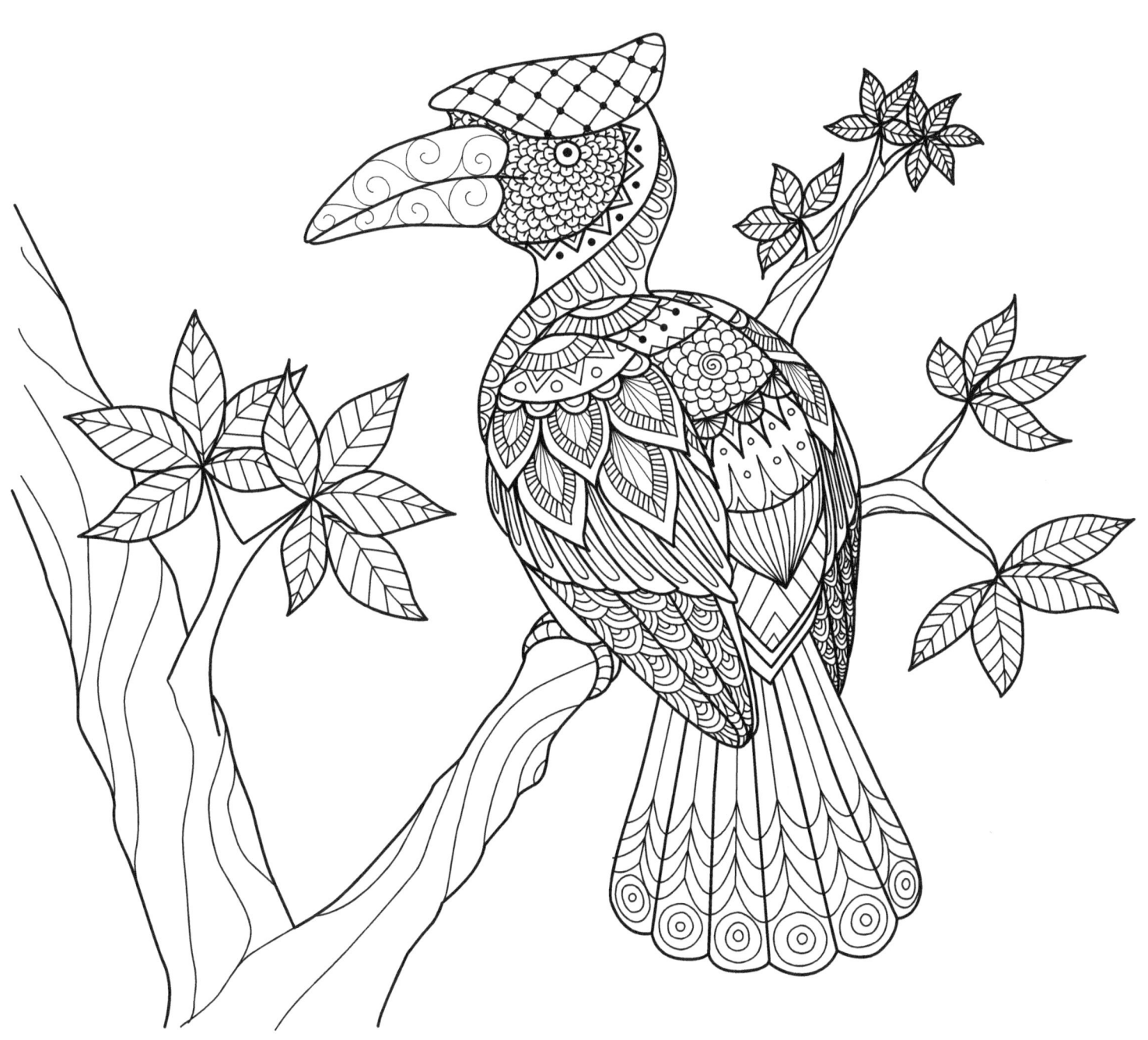

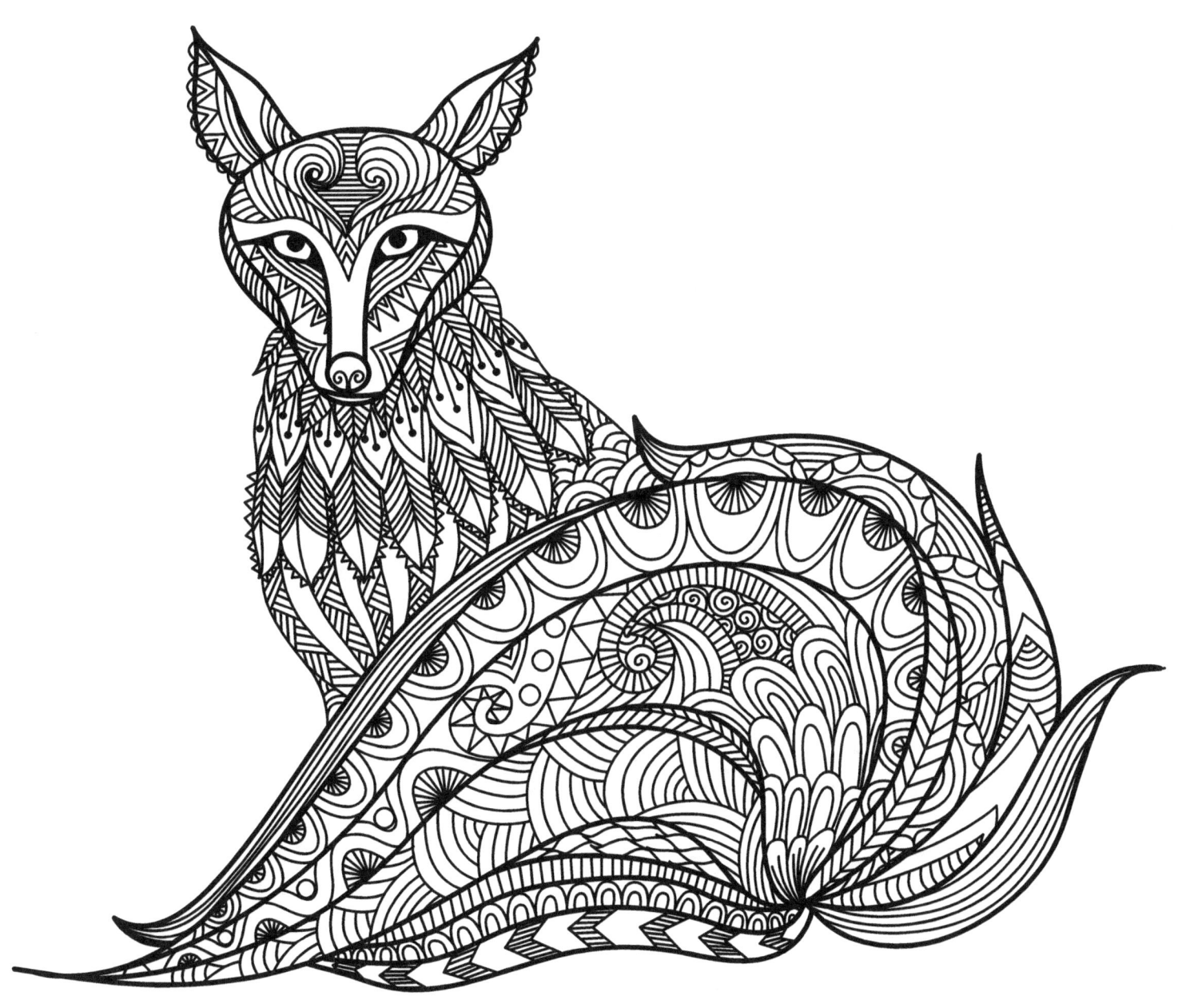

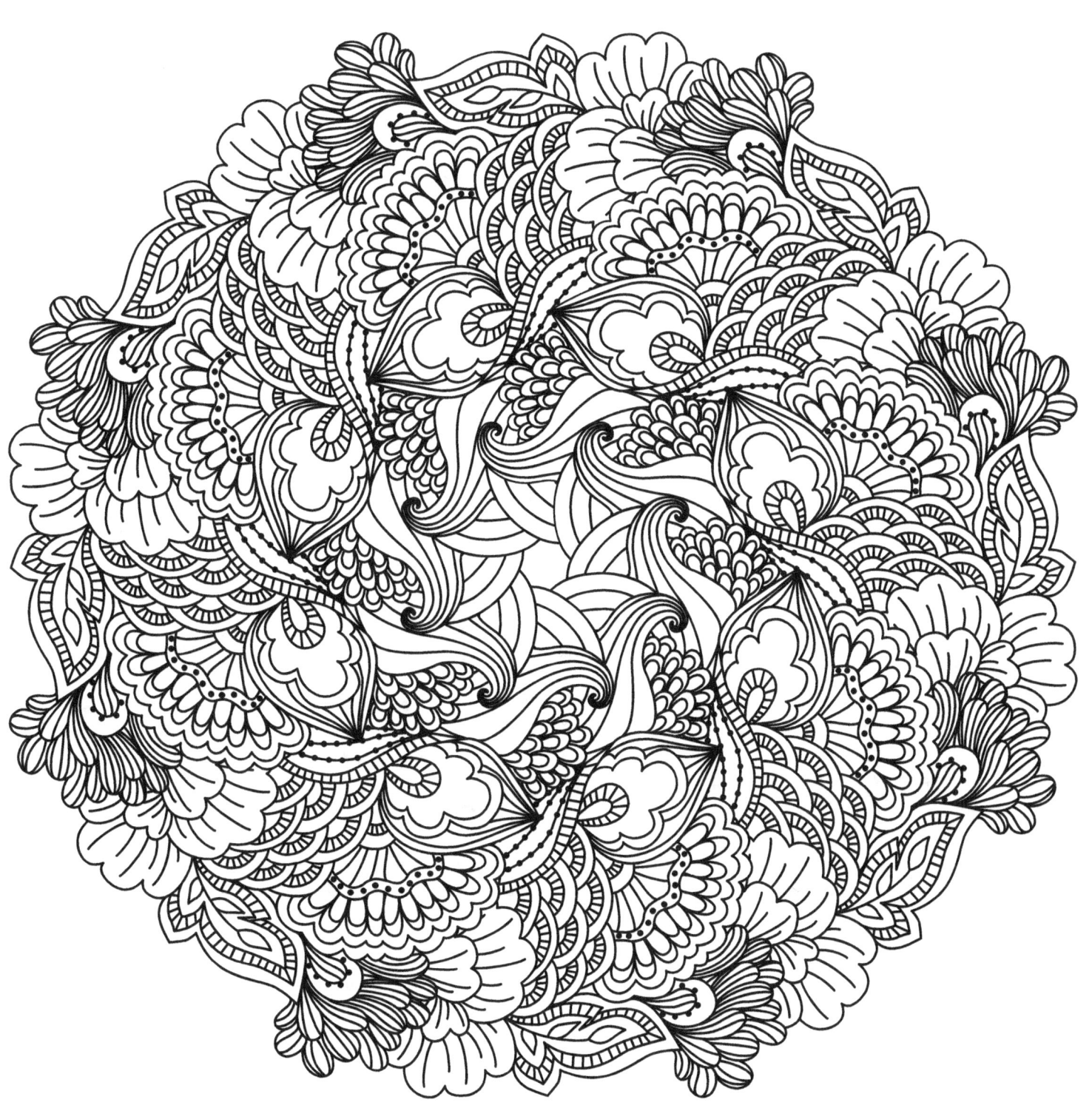

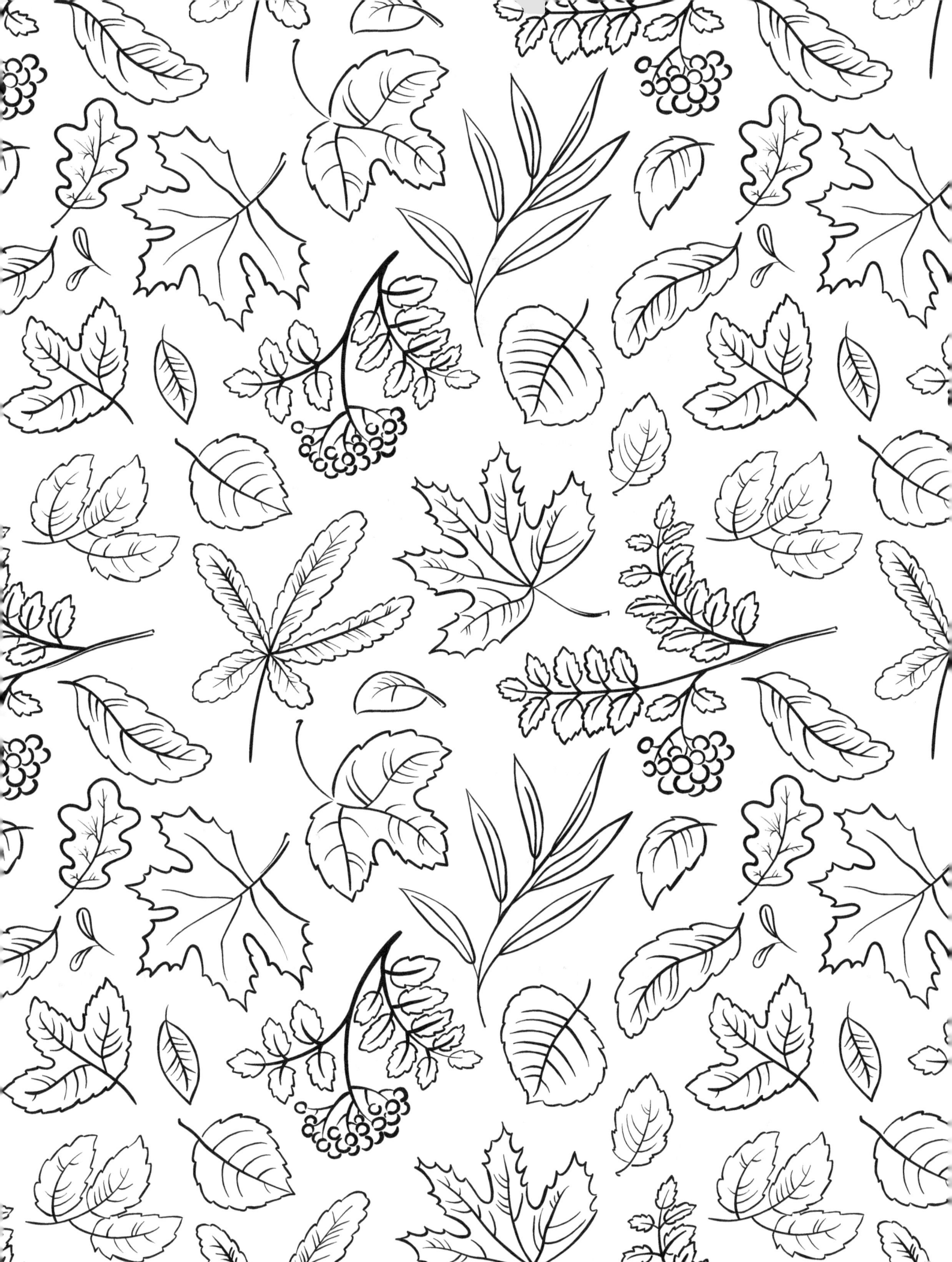

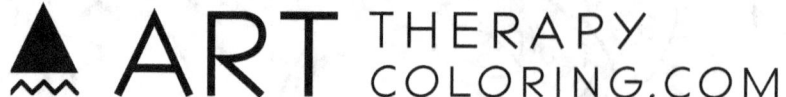

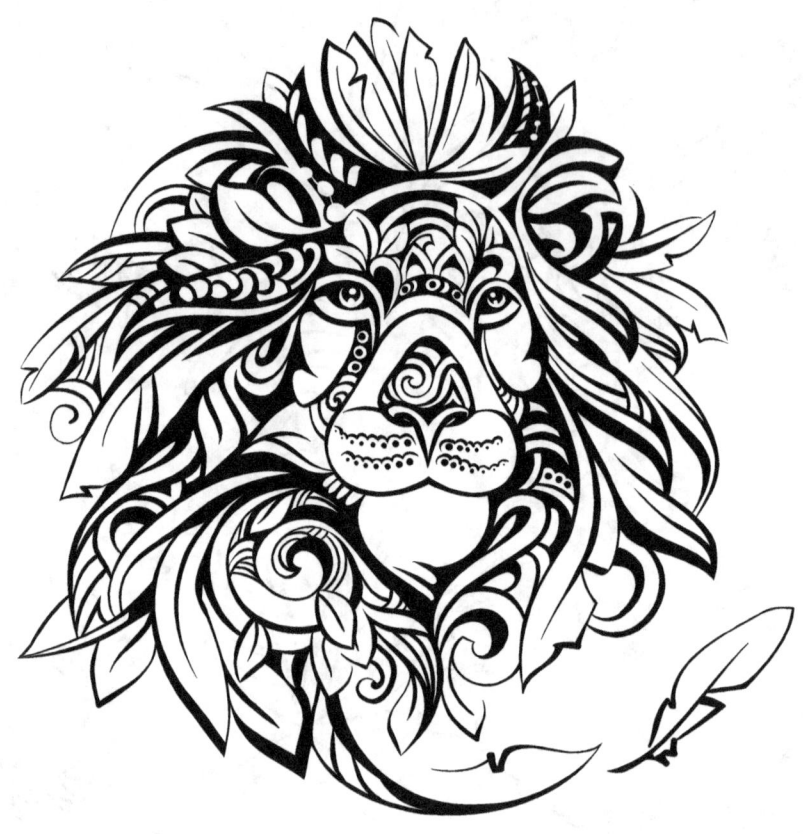

Did You Enjoy Our Coloring Book?

We Want To Hear About It!

Help spread the word about our coloring books! The best way to spread the word is through reviews. We know how busy you are, especially with all of that coloring, but we would appreciate it!

Visit our website at www.arttherapycoloring.com

Over 200 Art Therapy Coloring Books

See our collection of over 200 Art Therapy Coloring Books for Adults, Men, Women, Seniors, Teens, Kids, Boys, and Girls.

Coloring Books For Adults

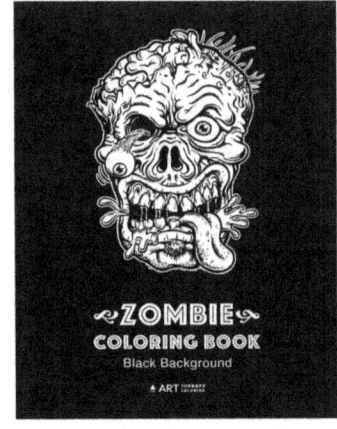

ZOMBIE
COLORING BOOK
Black Background

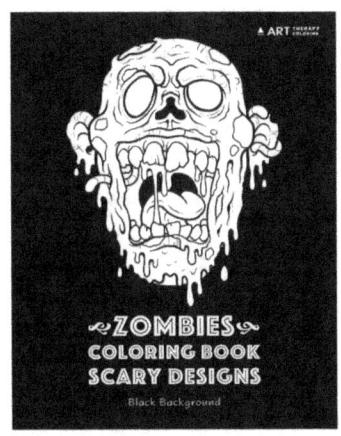

ZOMBIES
COLORING BOOK
SCARY DESIGNS
Black Background

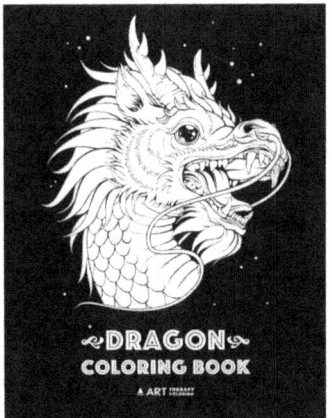

DRAGON
COLORING BOOK

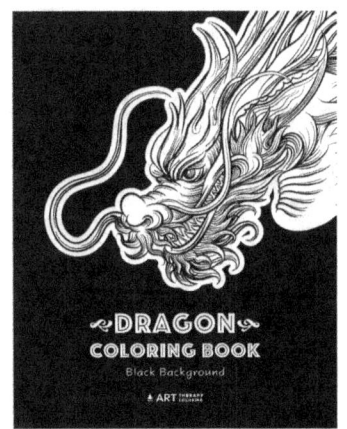

DRAGON
COLORING BOOK
Black Background

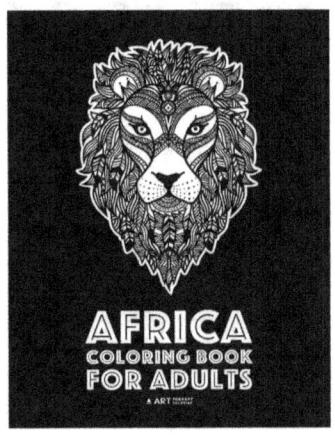

AFRICA
COLORING BOOK
FOR ADULTS

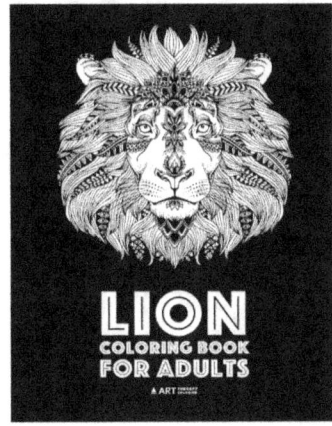

LION
COLORING BOOK
FOR ADULTS

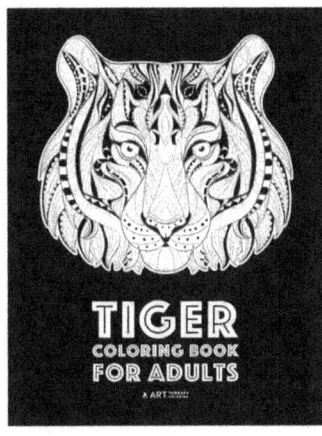

TIGER
COLORING BOOK
FOR ADULTS

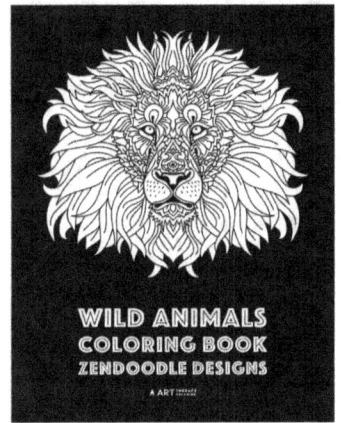

WILD ANIMALS
COLORING BOOK
ZENDOODLE DESIGNS

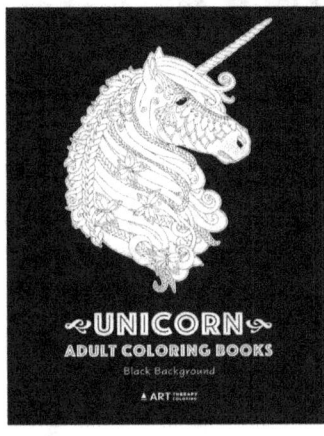

UNICORN
ADULT COLORING BOOKS
Black Background

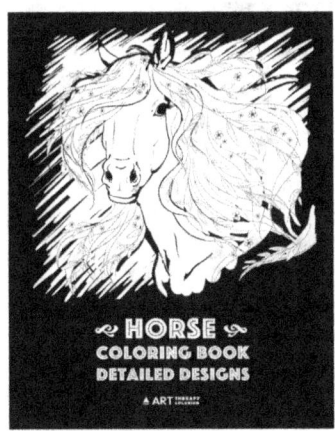

HORSE
COLORING BOOKS
DETAILED DESIGNS

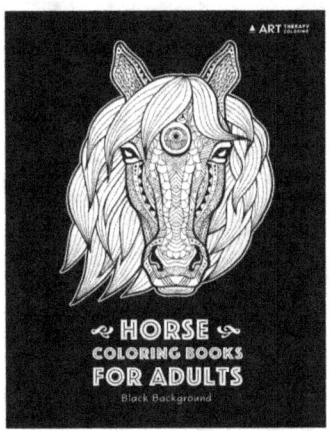

HORSE
COLORING BOOK
FOR ADULTS
Black Background

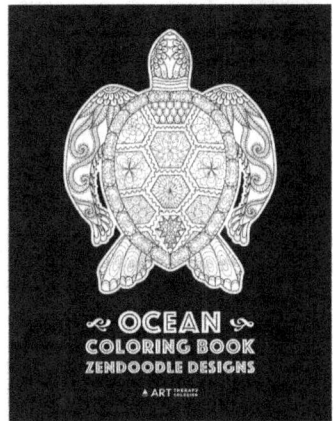

OCEAN
COLORING BOOK
ZENDOODLE DESIGNS

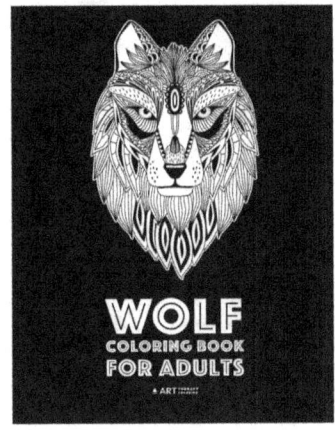

WOLF
COLORING BOOK
FOR ADULTS

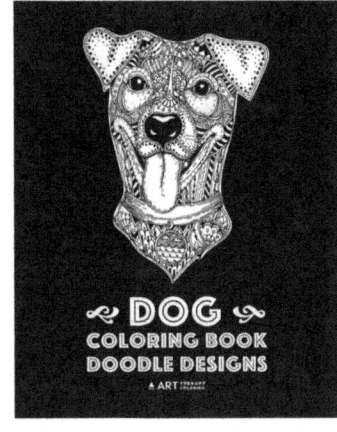

DOG
COLORING BOOK
DOODLE DESIGNS

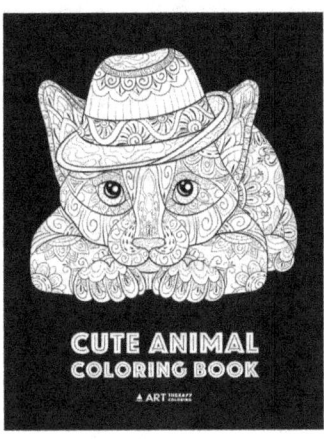

CUTE ANIMAL
COLORING BOOK

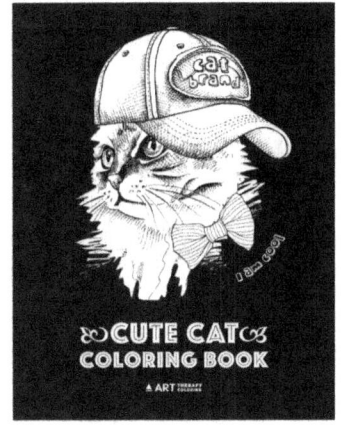

CUTE CAT
COLORING BOOK

Coloring Books For Adults

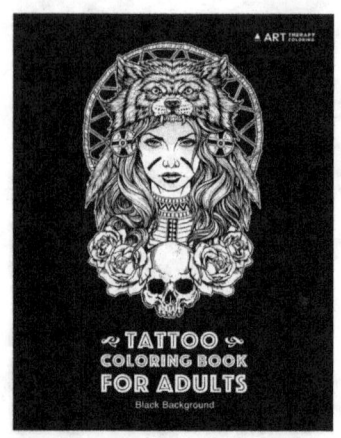

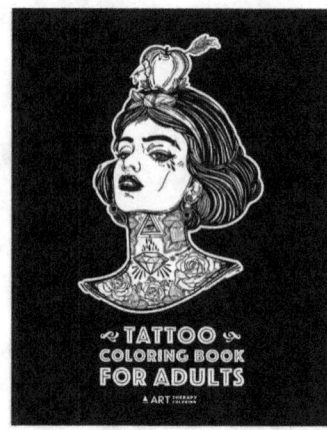

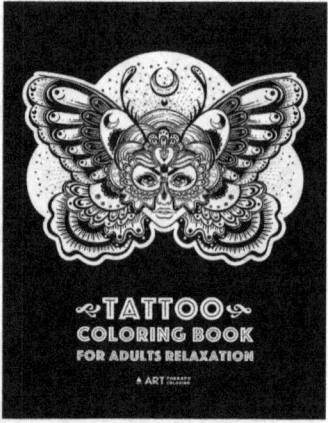

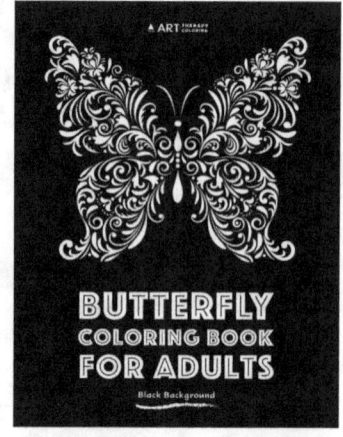

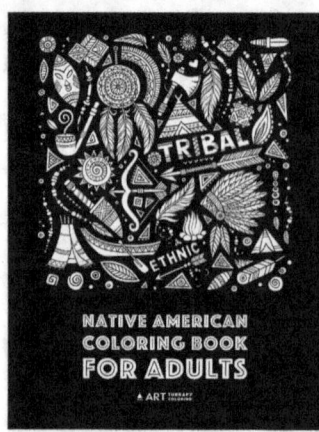

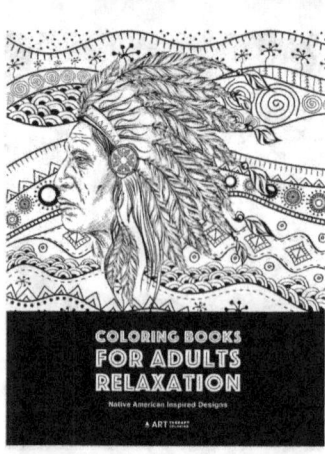

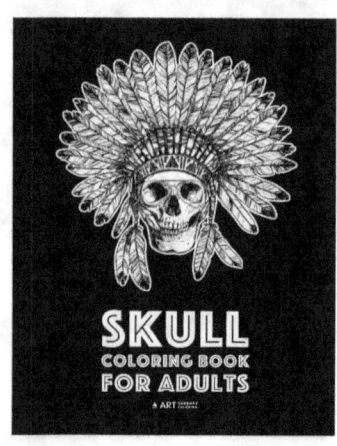

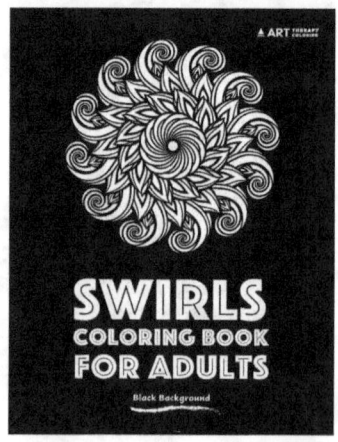

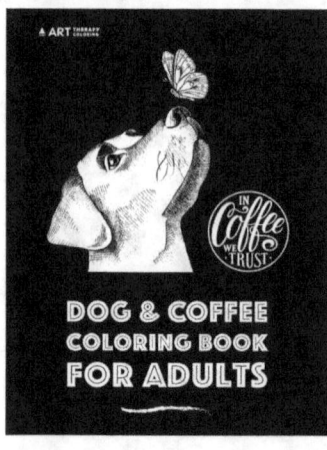

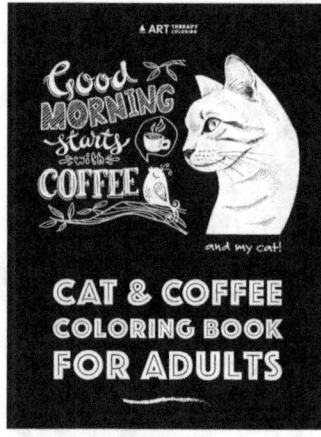

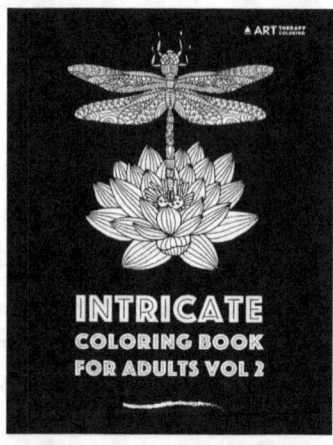

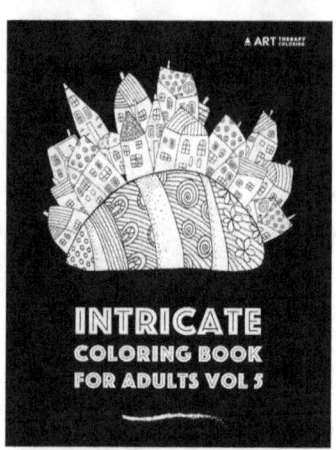

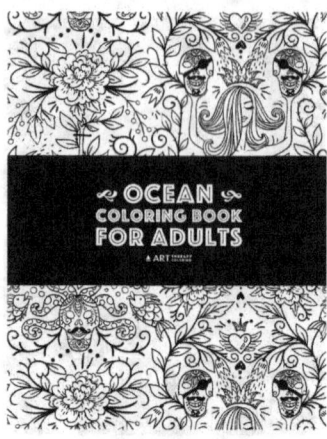

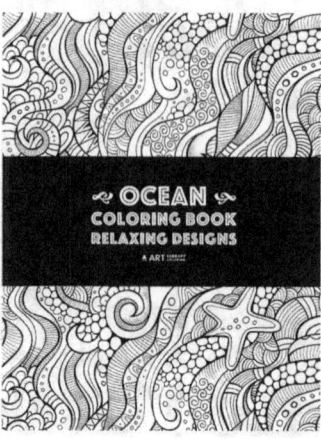

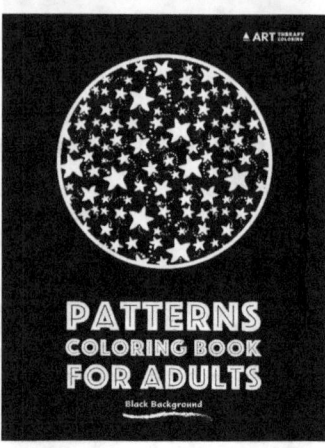

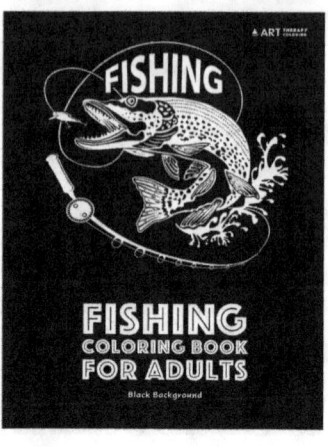

Coloring Books For Adults

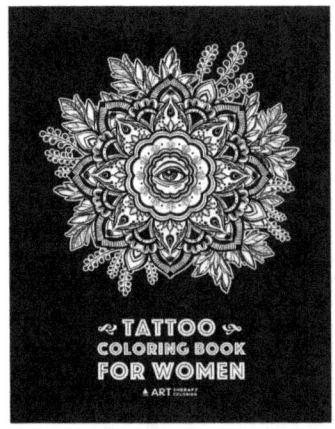

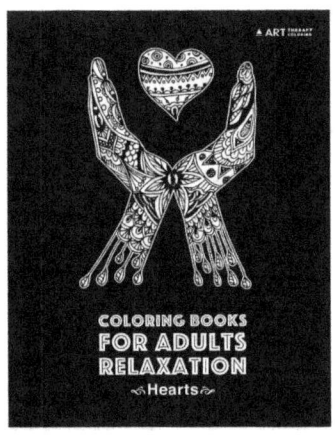

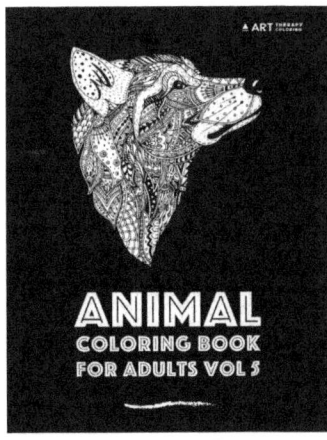

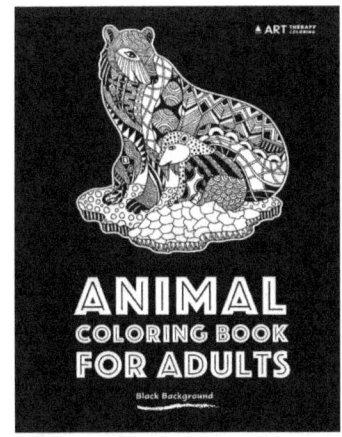

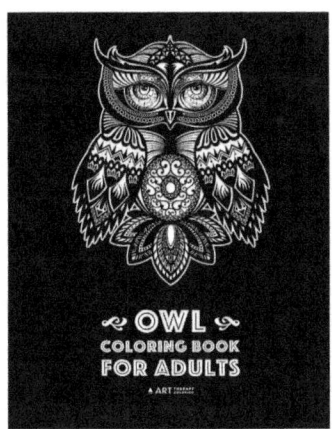

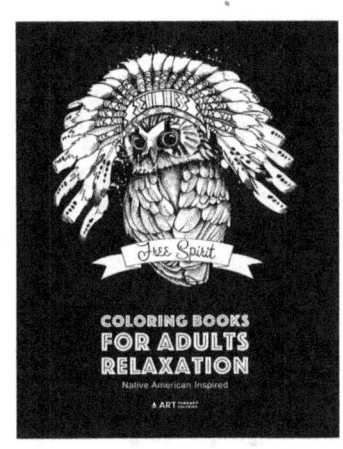

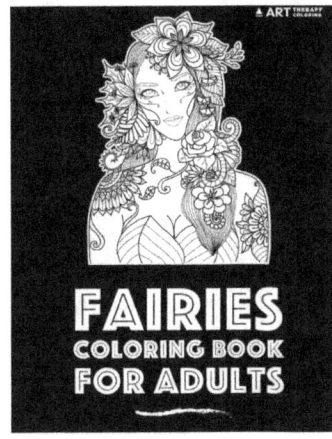

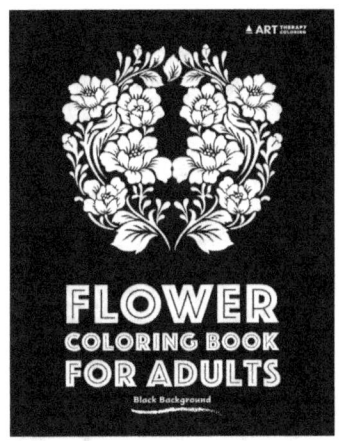

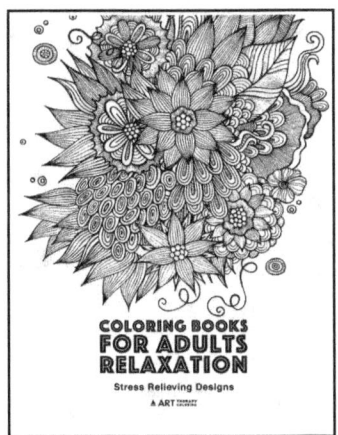

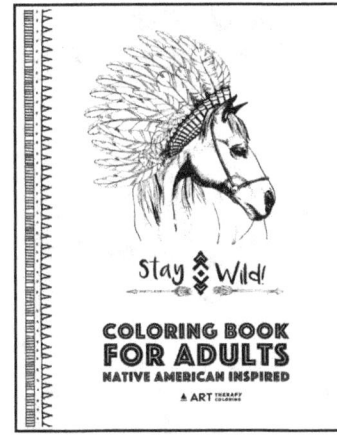

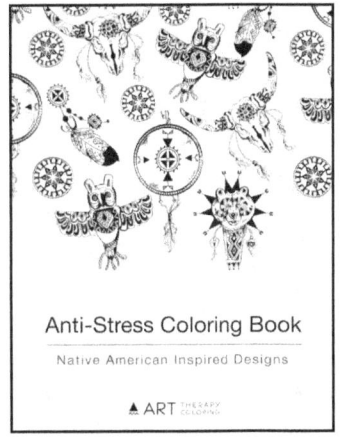

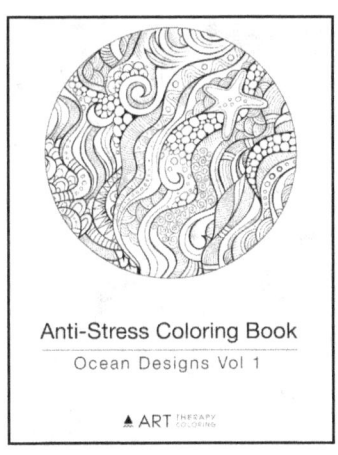

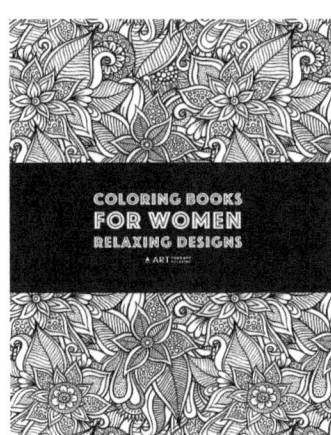

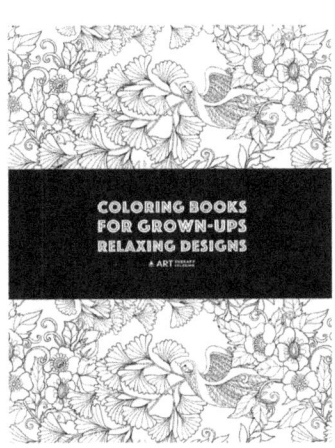

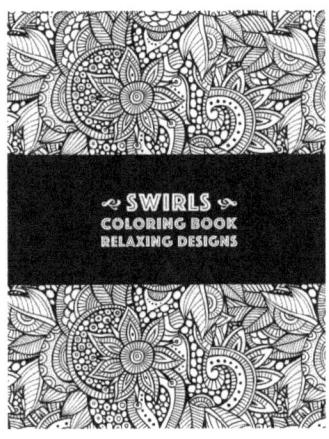

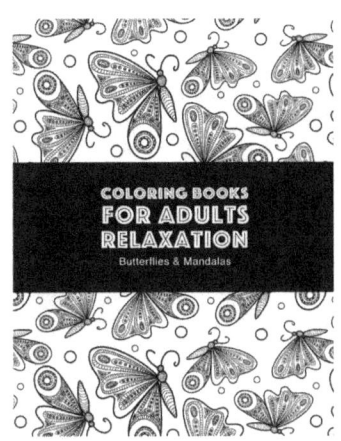

Coloring Books For Men

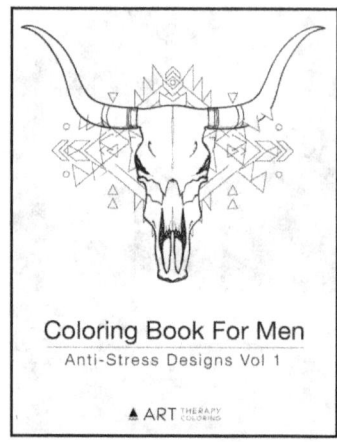

Coloring Book For Men
Anti-Stress Designs Vol 1

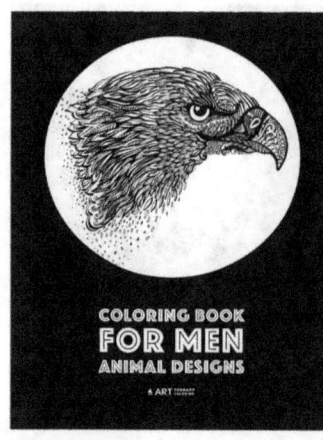

COLORING BOOK FOR MEN ANIMAL DESIGNS

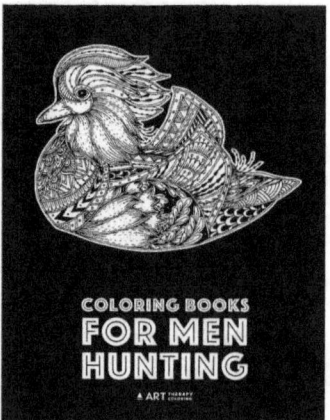

COLORING BOOKS FOR MEN HUNTING

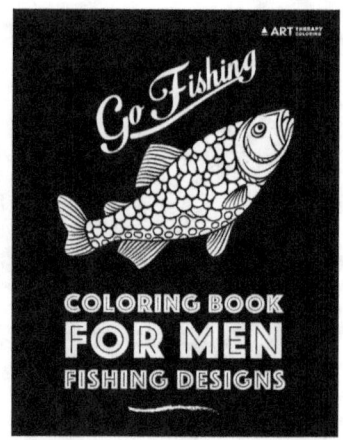

COLORING BOOK FOR MEN FISHING DESIGNS

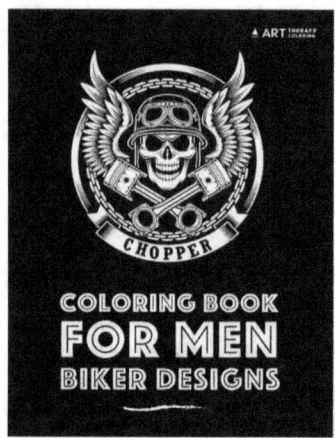

COLORING BOOK FOR MEN BIKER DESIGNS

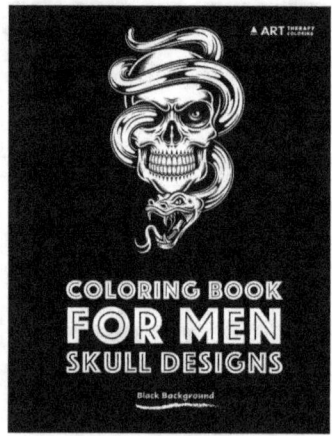

COLORING BOOK FOR MEN SKULL DESIGNS
Black Background

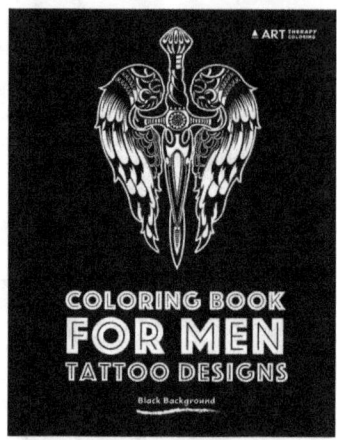

COLORING BOOK FOR MEN TATTOO DESIGNS
Black Background

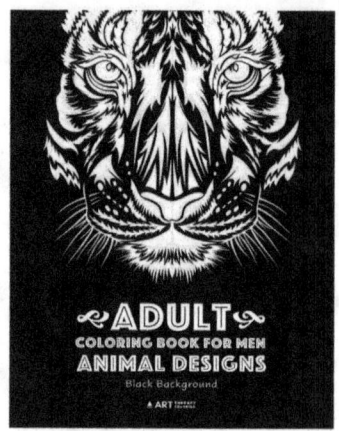

ADULT COLORING BOOK FOR MEN ANIMAL DESIGNS
Black Background

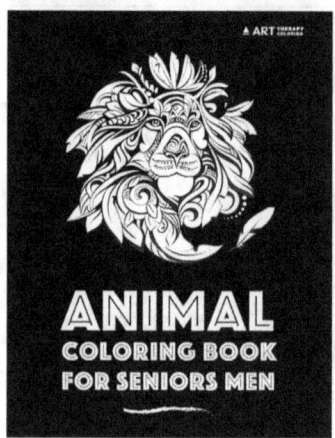

ANIMAL COLORING BOOK FOR SENIORS MEN

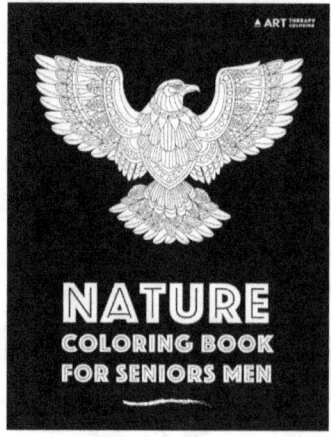

NATURE COLORING BOOK FOR SENIORS MEN

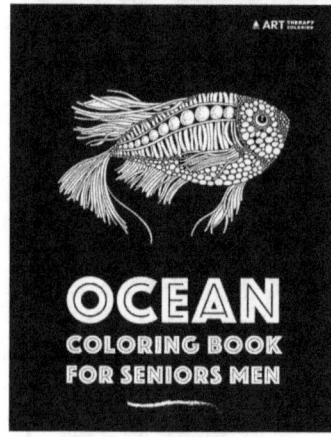

OCEAN COLORING BOOK FOR SENIORS MEN

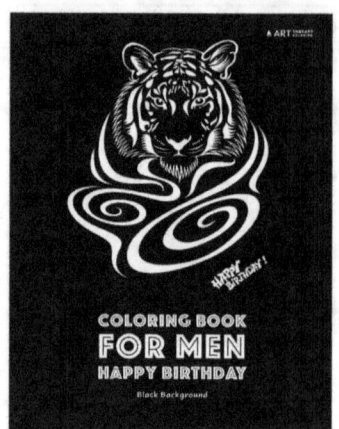

COLORING BOOK FOR MEN HAPPY BIRTHDAY
Black Background

Coloring Books For Seniors

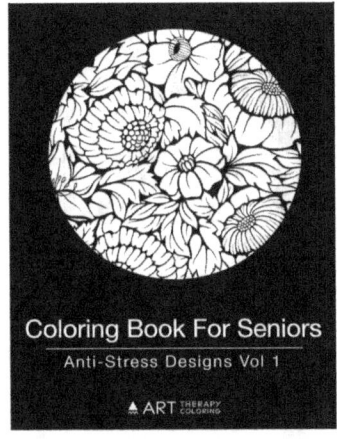

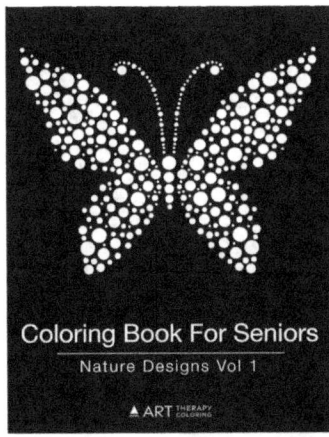

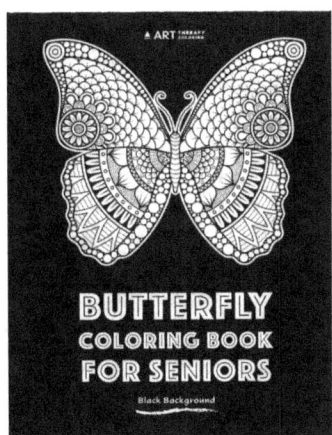

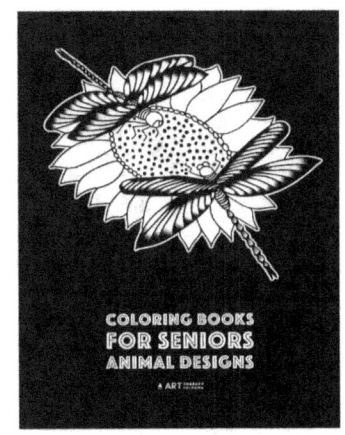

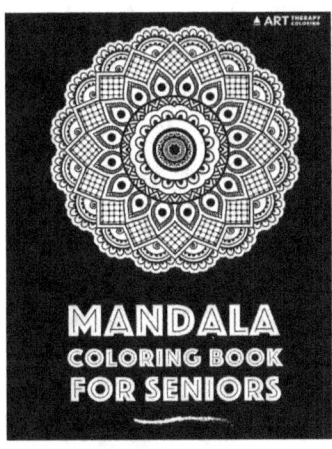

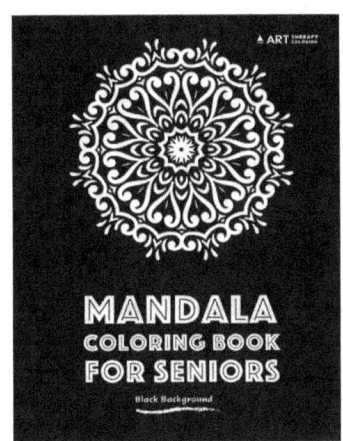

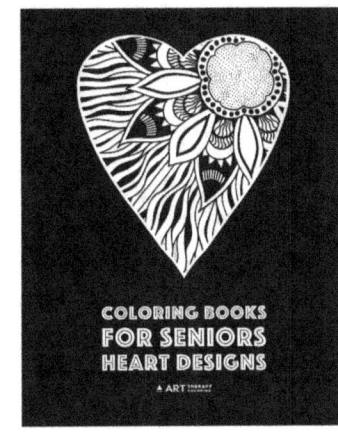

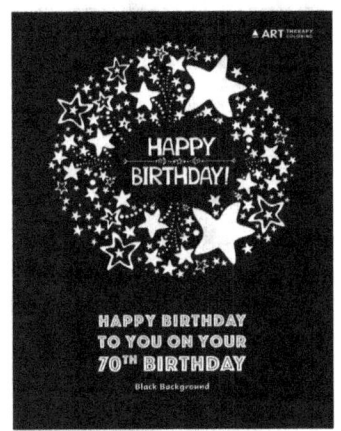

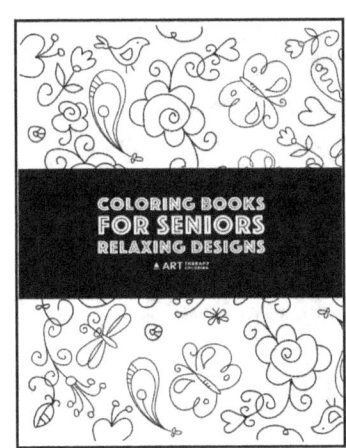

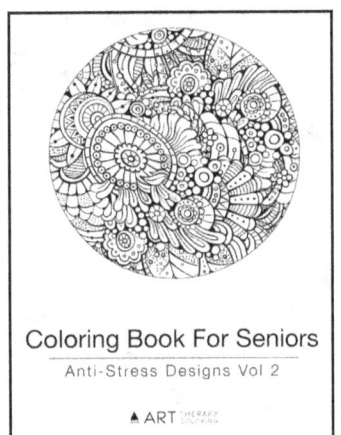

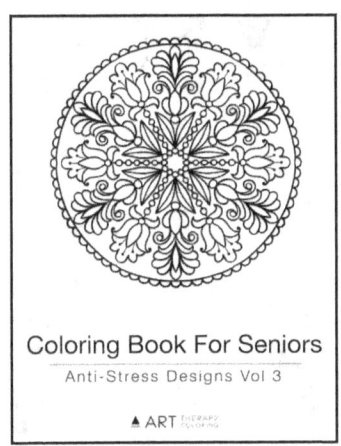

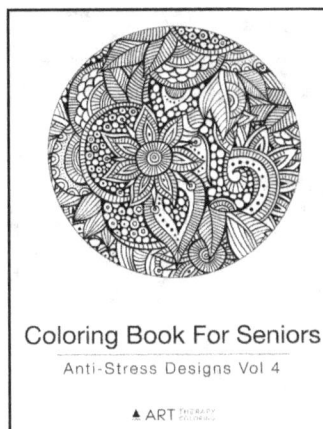

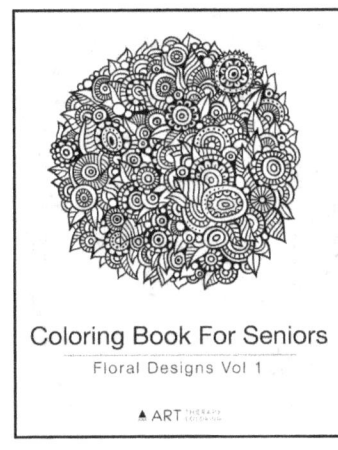

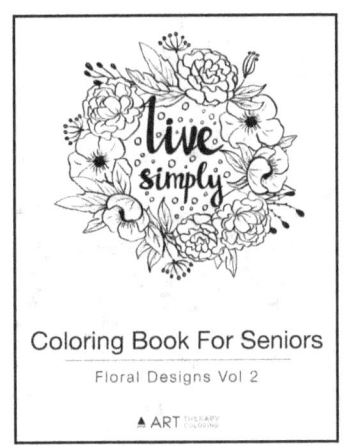

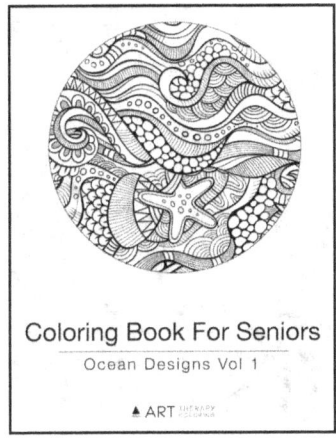

Coloring Books For Teens

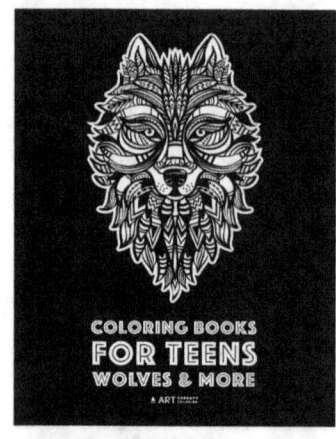

COLORING BOOKS FOR TEENS WOLVES & MORE

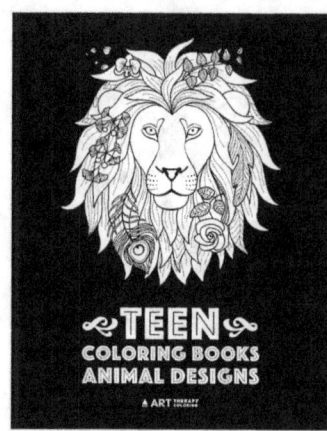

TEEN COLORING BOOKS ANIMAL DESIGNS

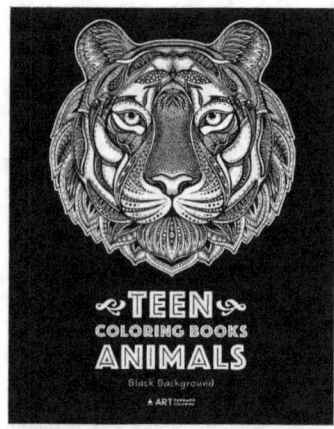

TEEN COLORING BOOKS ANIMALS Black Background

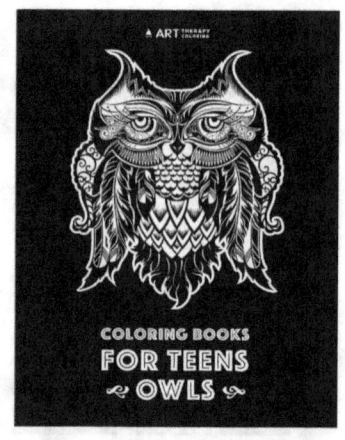

COLORING BOOKS FOR TEENS OWLS

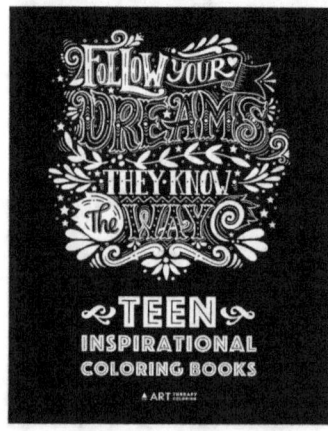

TEEN INSPIRATIONAL COLORING BOOKS

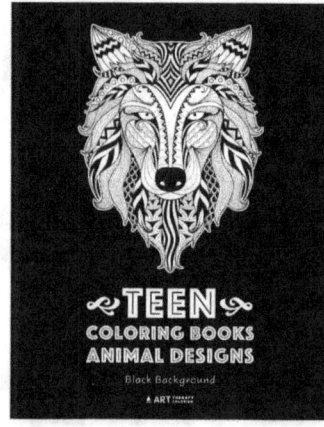

TEEN COLORING BOOKS ANIMAL DESIGNS Black Background

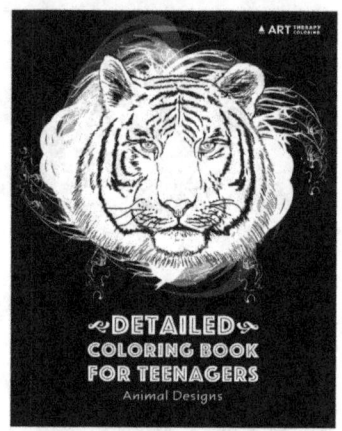

DETAILED COLORING BOOK FOR TEENAGERS Animal Designs

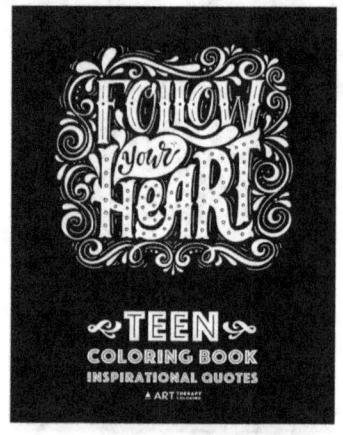

TEEN COLORING BOOK INSPIRATIONAL QUOTES

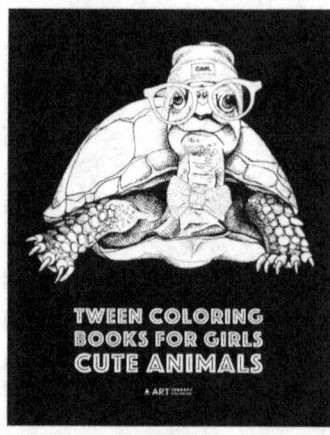

TWEEN COLORING BOOKS FOR GIRLS CUTE ANIMALS

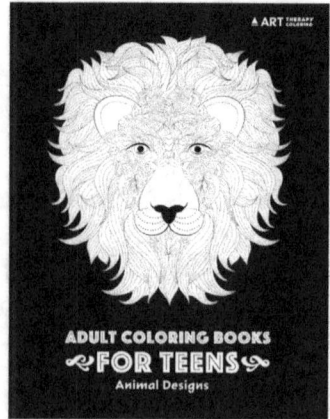

ADULT COLORING BOOKS FOR TEENS Animal Designs

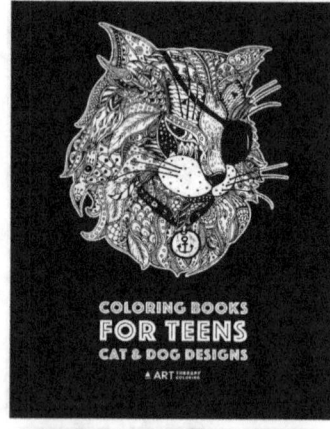

COLORING BOOKS FOR TEENS CAT & DOG DESIGNS

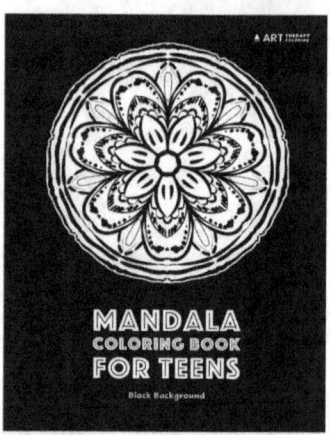

MANDALA COLORING BOOK FOR TEENS Black Background

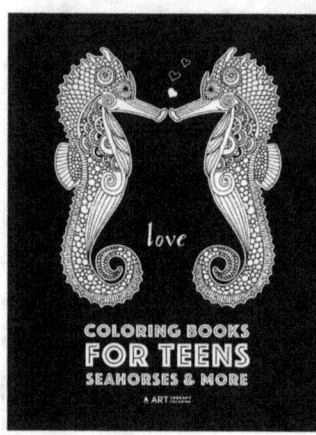

COLORING BOOKS FOR TEENS SEAHORSES & MORE

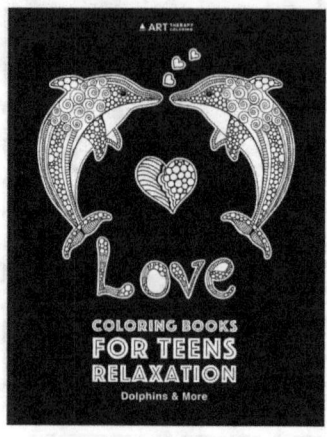

COLORING BOOKS FOR TEENS RELAXATION Dolphins & More

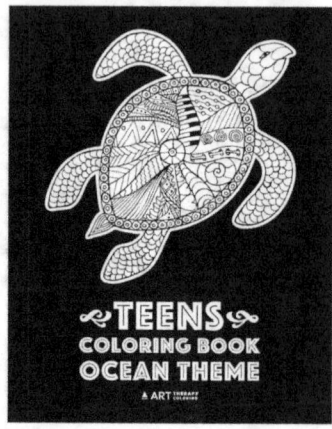

TEENS COLORING BOOK OCEAN THEME

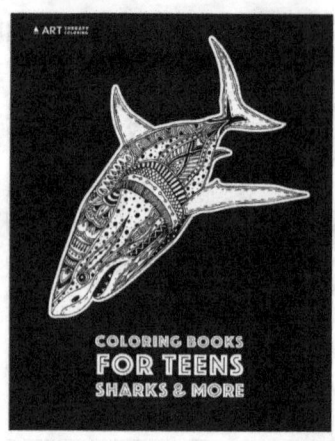

COLORING BOOKS FOR TEENS SHARKS & MORE

Coloring Books For Teens

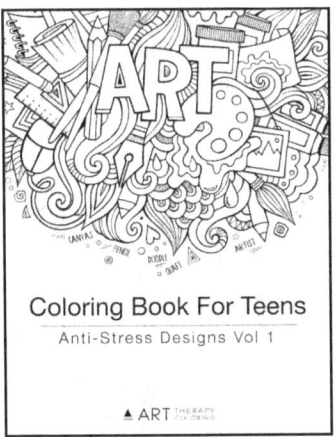

Coloring Book For Teens

Anti-Stress Designs Vol 1

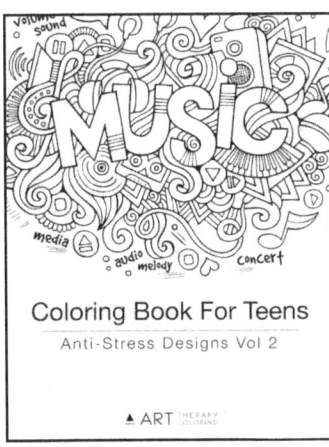

Coloring Book For Teens

Anti-Stress Designs Vol 2

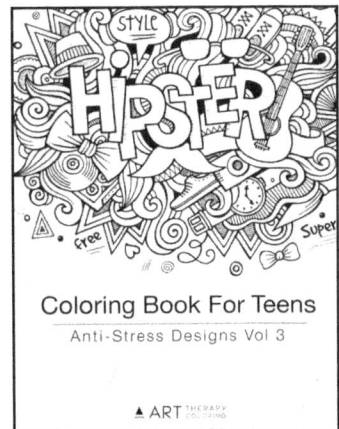

Coloring Book For Teens

Anti-Stress Designs Vol 3

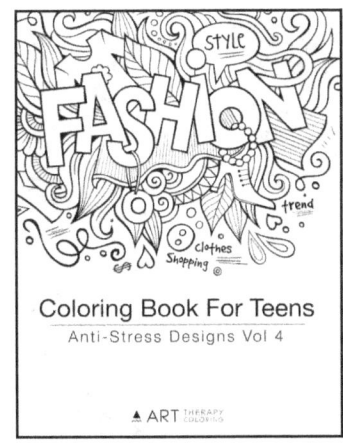

Coloring Book For Teens

Anti-Stress Designs Vol 4

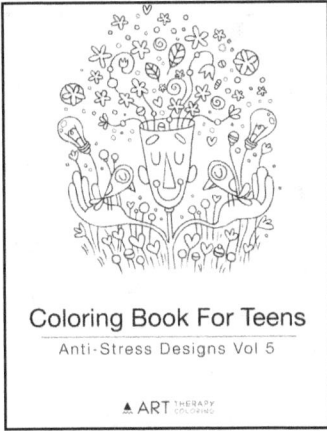

Coloring Book For Teens

Anti-Stress Designs Vol 5

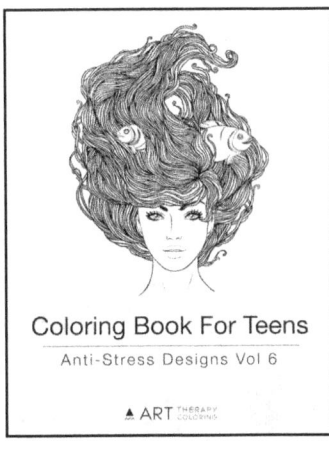

Coloring Book For Teens

Anti-Stress Designs Vol 6

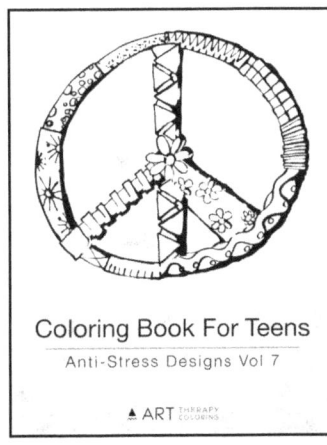

Coloring Book For Teens

Anti-Stress Designs Vol 7

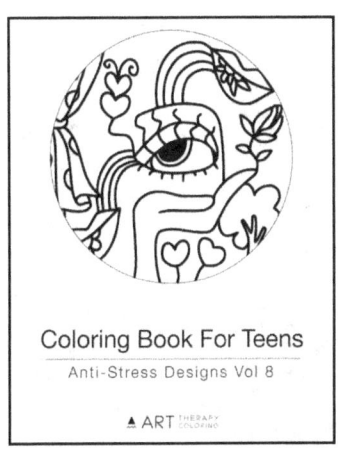

Coloring Book For Teens

Anti-Stress Designs Vol 8

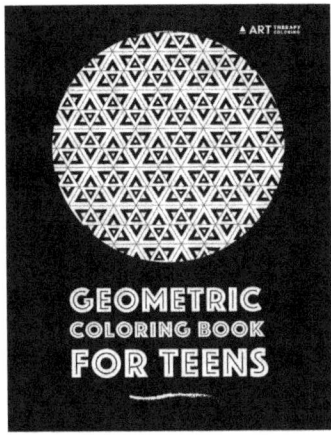

GEOMETRIC COLORING BOOK FOR TEENS

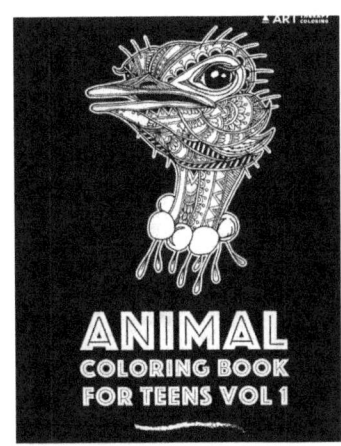

ANIMAL COLORING BOOK FOR TEENS VOL 1

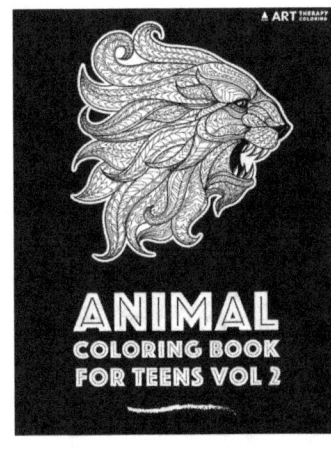

ANIMAL COLORING BOOK FOR TEENS VOL 2

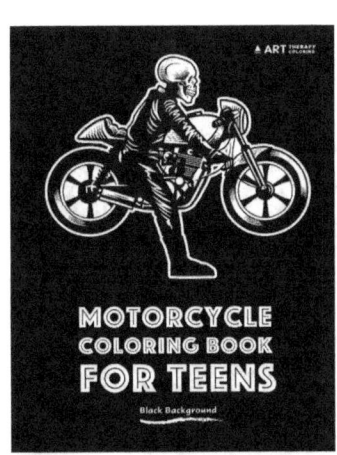

MOTORCYCLE COLORING BOOK FOR TEENS

Black Background

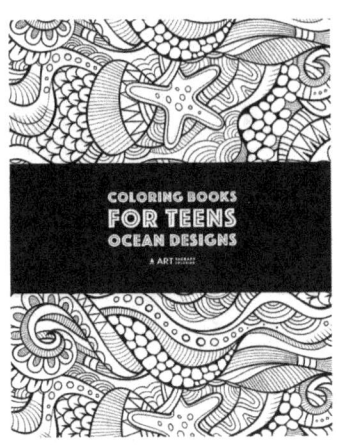

COLORING BOOKS FOR TEENS OCEAN DESIGNS

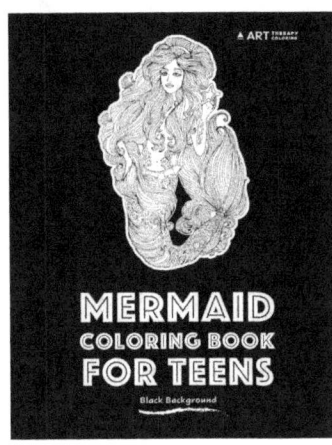

MERMAID COLORING BOOK FOR TEENS

Black Background

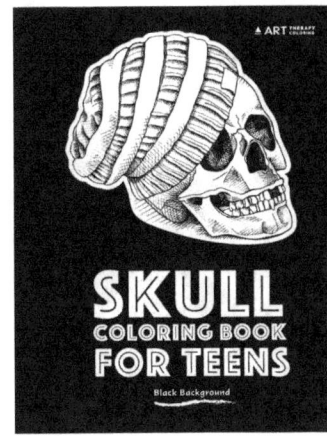

SKULL COLORING BOOK FOR TEENS

Black Background

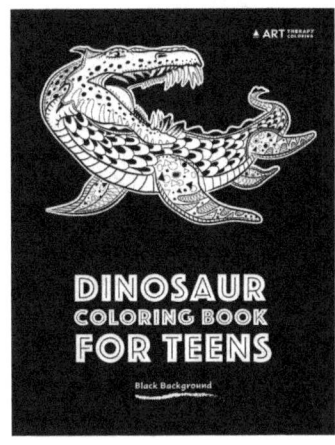

DINOSAUR COLORING BOOK FOR TEENS

Black Background

Coloring Books For Girls

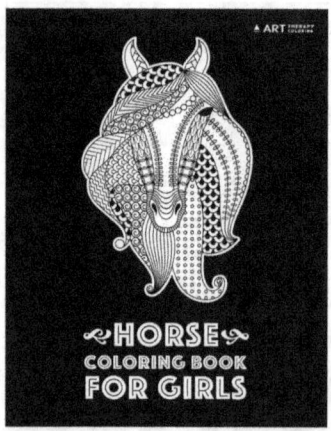

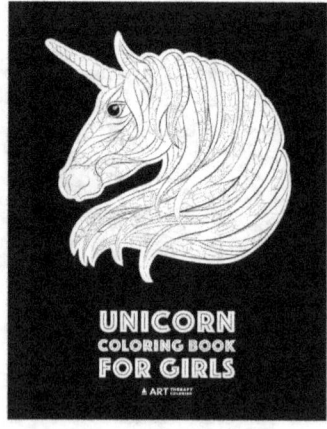

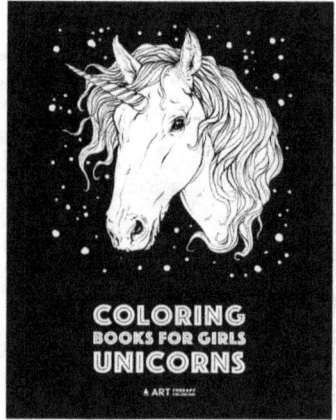

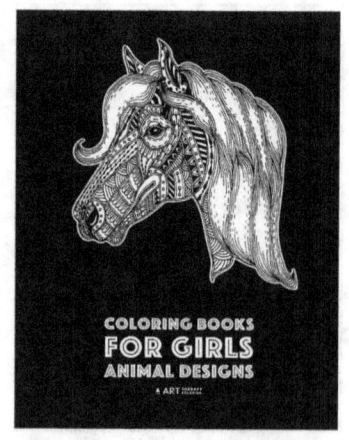

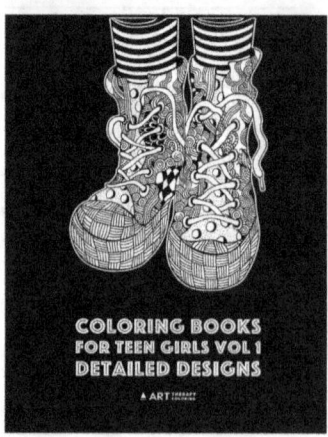

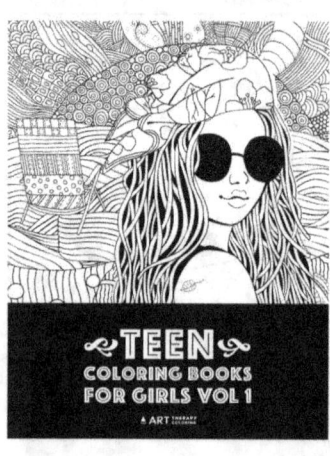

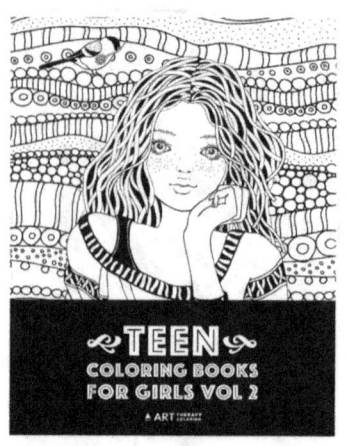

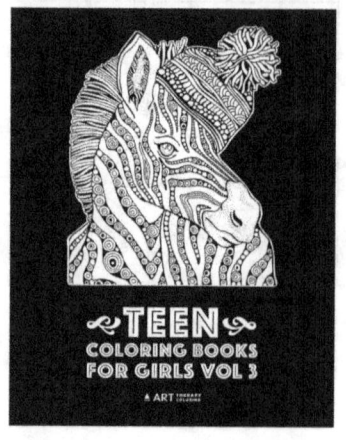

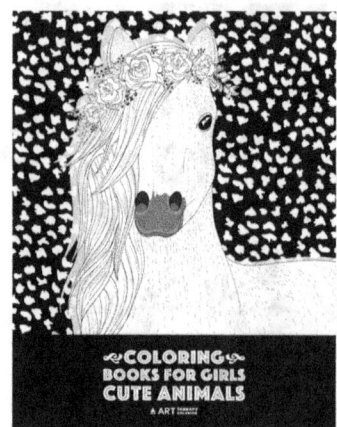

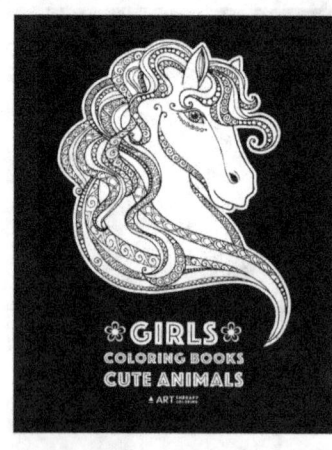

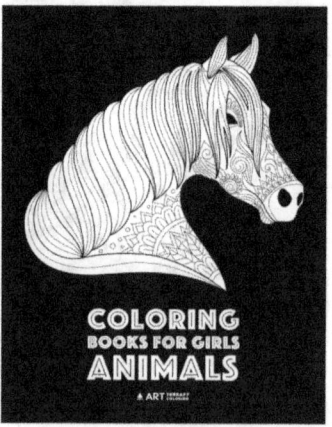

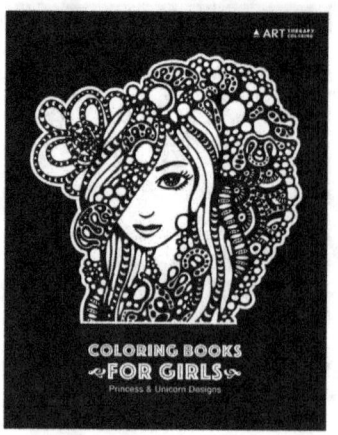

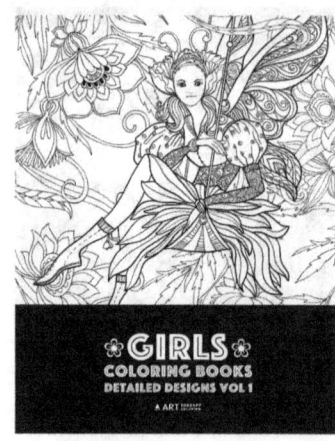

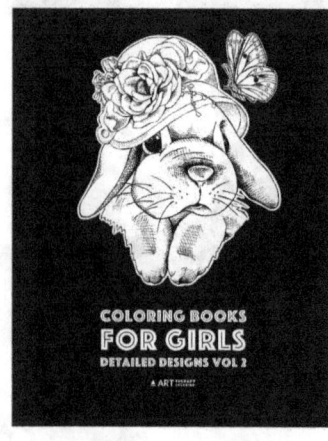

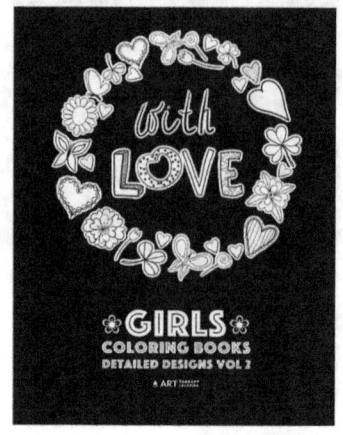

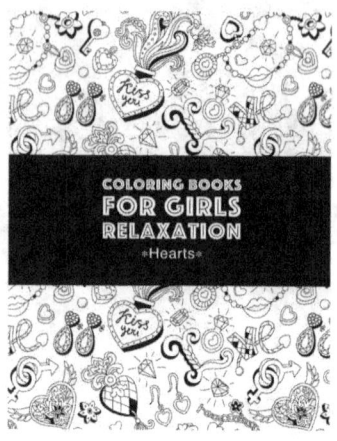

Art Therapy Coloring Books

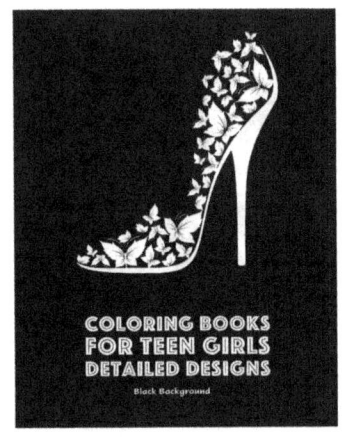

COLORING BOOKS
FOR TEEN GIRLS
DETAILED DESIGNS
Black Background

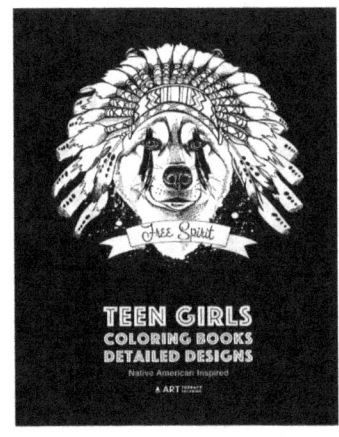

TEEN GIRLS
COLORING BOOKS
DETAILED DESIGNS
Native American Inspired

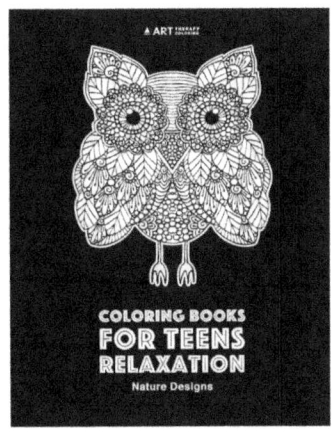

COLORING BOOKS
FOR TEENS
RELAXATION
Nature Designs

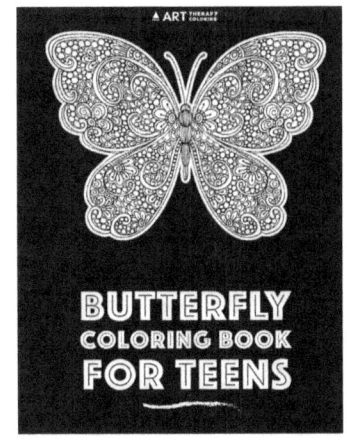

BUTTERFLY
COLORING BOOK
FOR TEENS

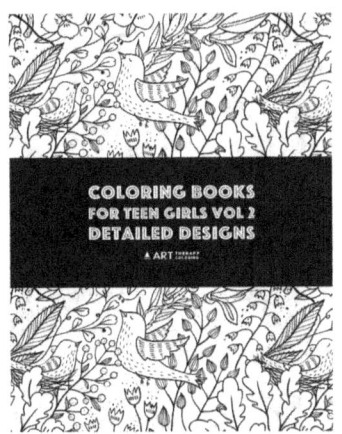

COLORING BOOKS
FOR TEEN GIRLS VOL 2
DETAILED DESIGNS

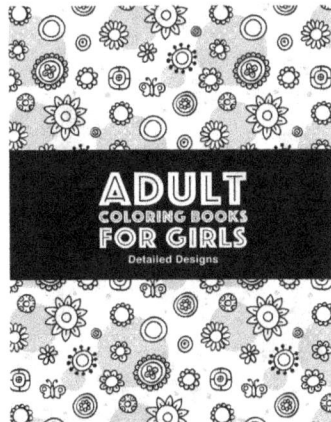

ADULT
COLORING BOOKS
FOR GIRLS
Detailed Designs

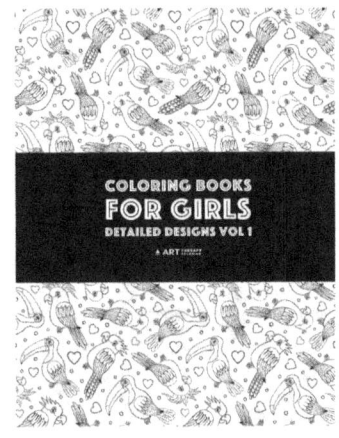

COLORING BOOKS
FOR GIRLS
DETAILED DESIGNS VOL 1

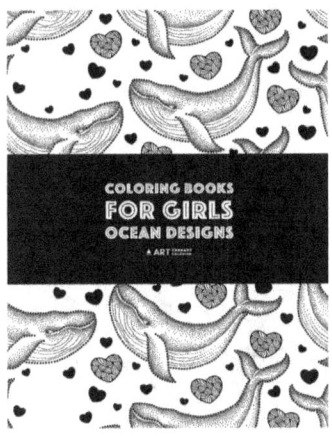

COLORING BOOKS
FOR GIRLS
OCEAN DESIGNS

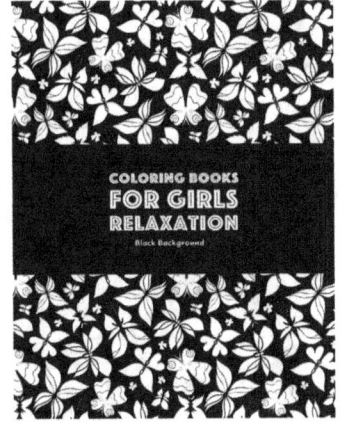

COLORING BOOKS
FOR GIRLS
RELAXATION
Black Background

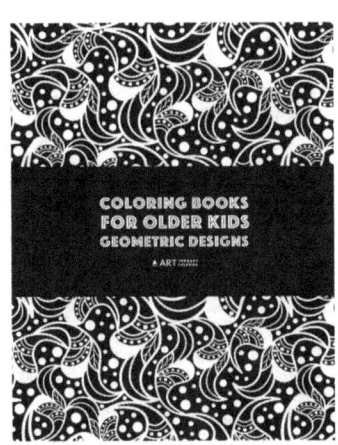

COLORING BOOKS
FOR OLDER KIDS
GEOMETRIC DESIGNS

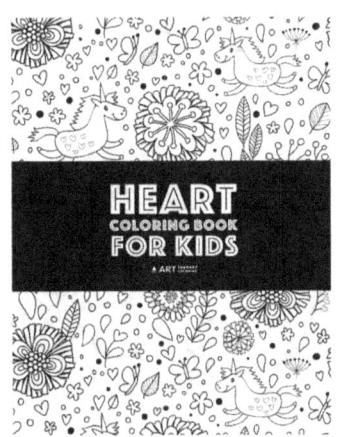

HEART
COLORING BOOK
FOR KIDS

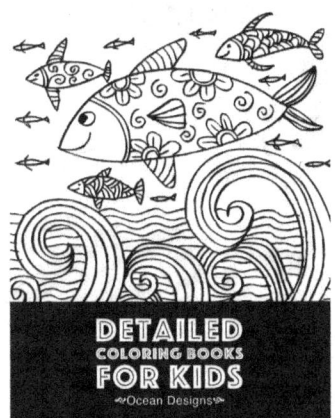

DETAILED
COLORING BOOKS
FOR KIDS
Ocean Designs

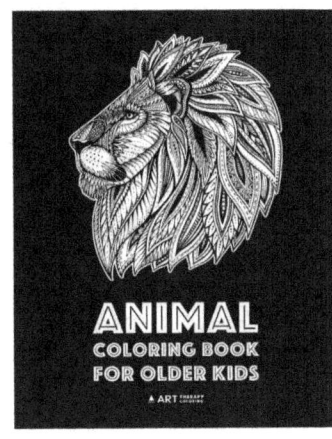

ANIMAL
COLORING BOOK
FOR OLDER KIDS

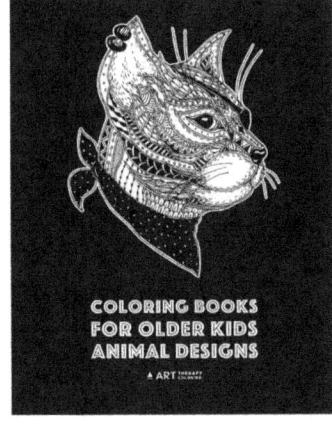

COLORING BOOKS
FOR OLDER KIDS
ANIMAL DESIGNS

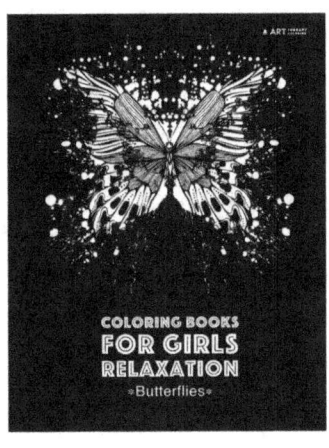

COLORING BOOKS
FOR GIRLS
RELAXATION
Butterflies

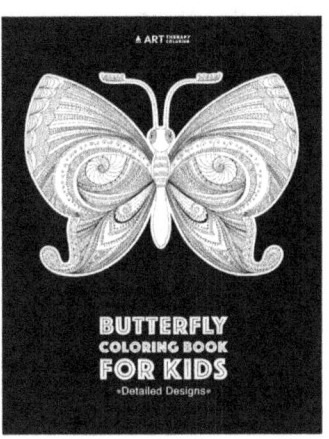

BUTTERFLY
COLORING BOOK
FOR KIDS
Detailed Designs

Coloring Books For Boys

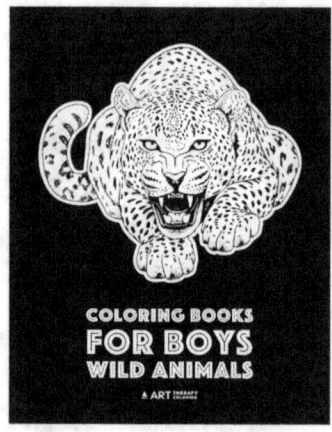

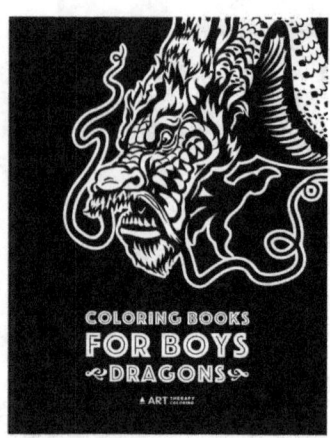

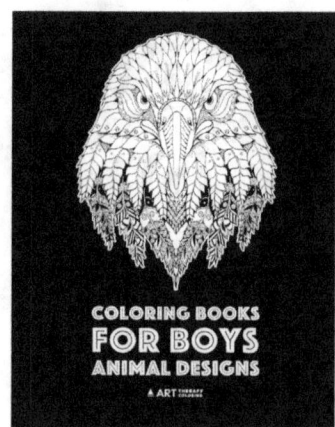

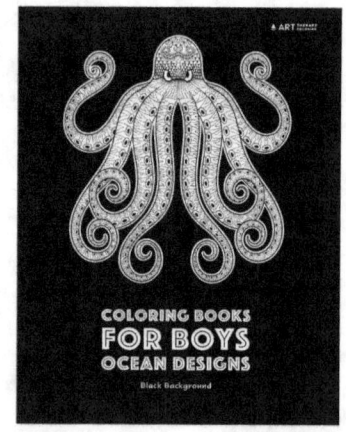

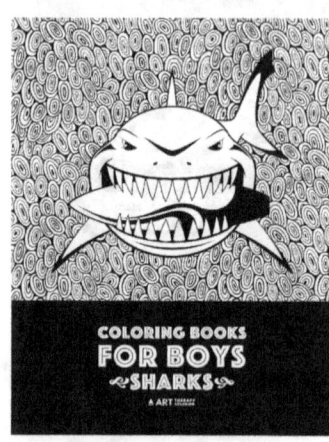

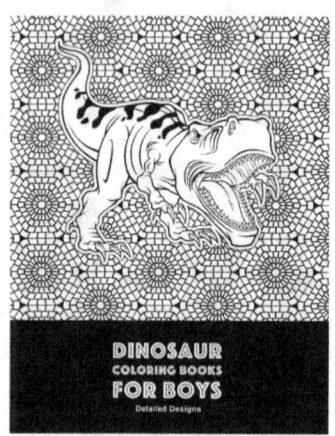

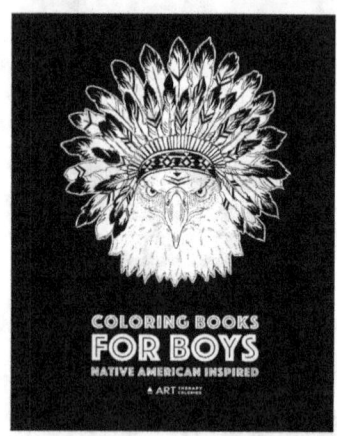

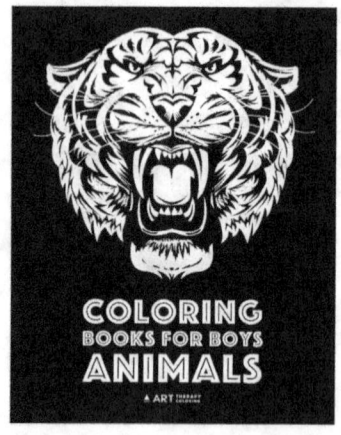

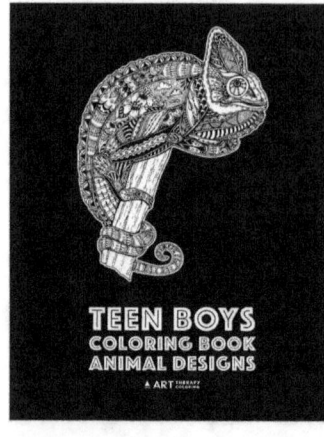

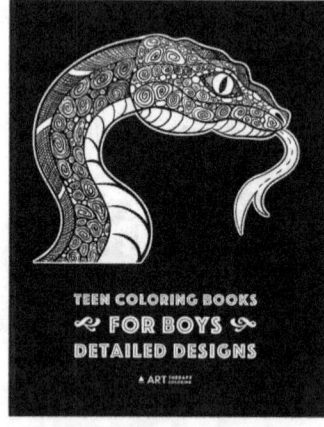

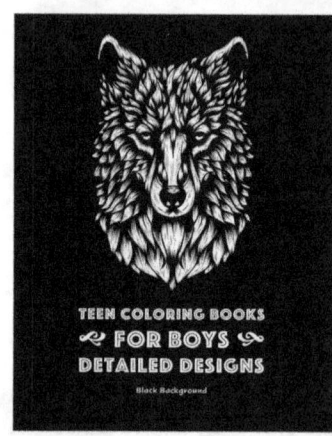

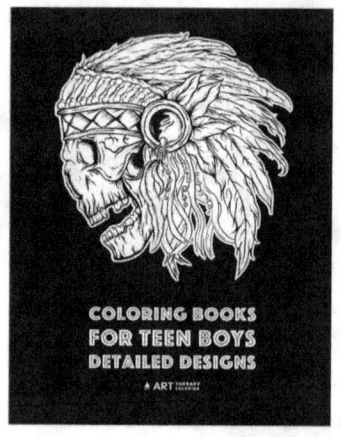

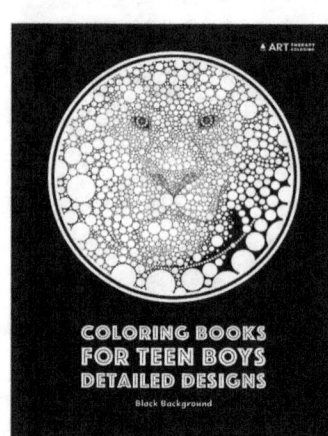

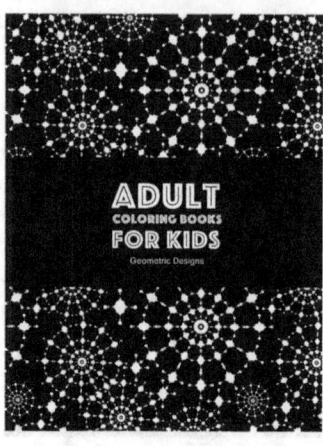

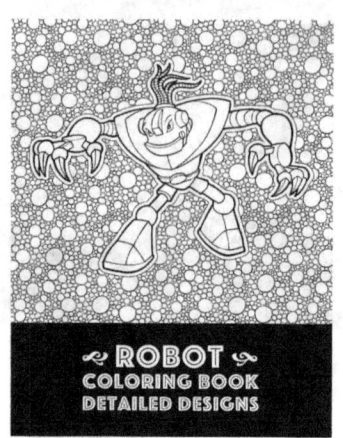

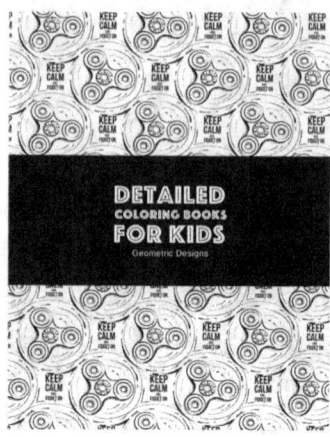

Coloring Books For Kids

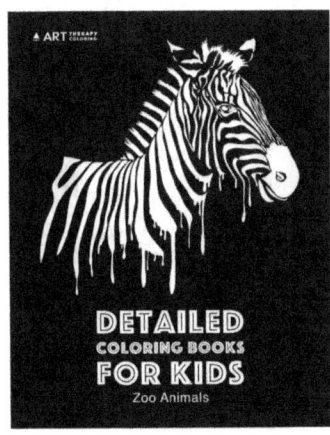

DETAILED
COLORING BOOKS
FOR KIDS
Zoo Animals

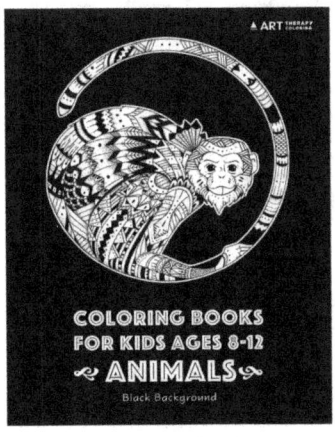

COLORING BOOKS
FOR KIDS AGES 8-12
ANIMALS
Black Background

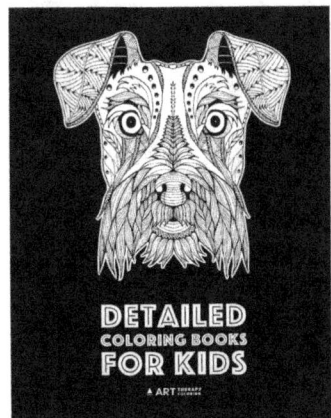

DETAILED
COLORING BOOKS
FOR KIDS

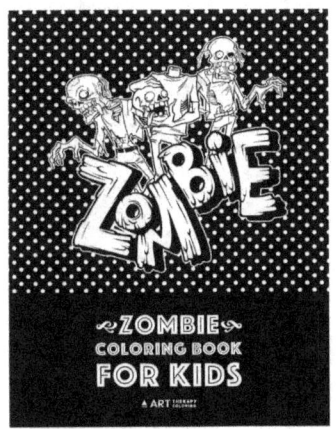

ZOMBIE
COLORING BOOK
FOR KIDS

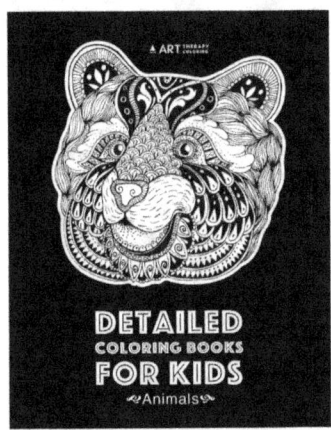

DETAILED
COLORING BOOKS
FOR KIDS
Animals

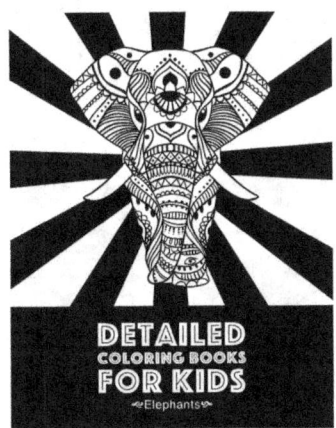

DETAILED
COLORING BOOKS
FOR KIDS
Elephants

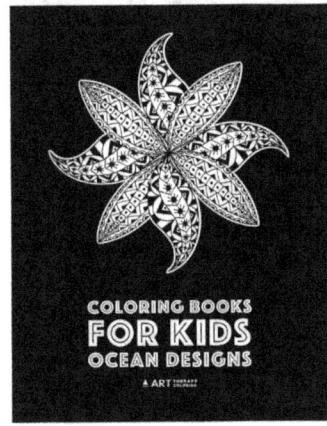

COLORING BOOKS
FOR KIDS
OCEAN DESIGNS

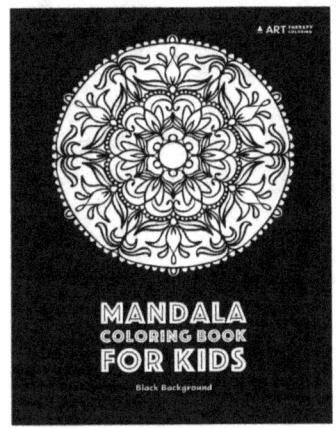

MANDALA
COLORING BOOK
FOR KIDS
Black Background

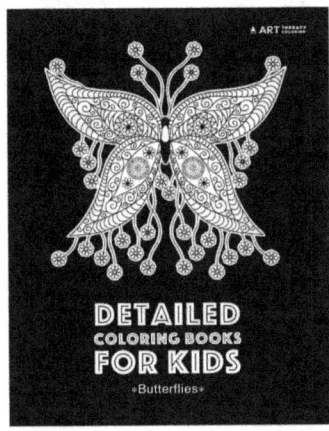

DETAILED
COLORING BOOKS
FOR KIDS
Butterflies

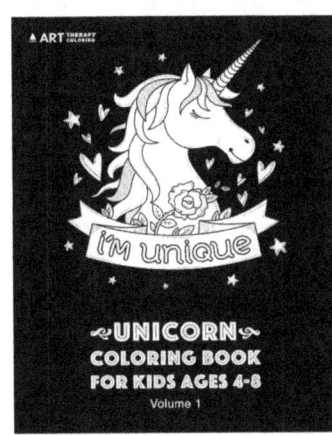

UNICORN
COLORING BOOK
FOR KIDS AGES 4-8
Volume 1

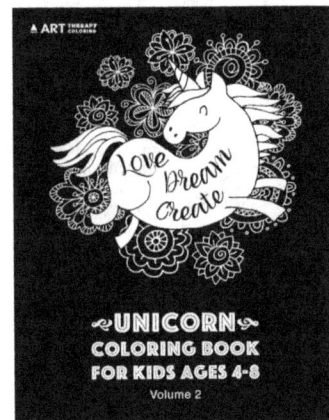

UNICORN
COLORING BOOK
FOR KIDS AGES 4-8
Volume 2

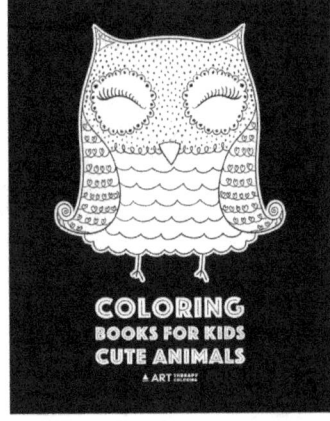

COLORING
BOOKS FOR KIDS
CUTE ANIMALS

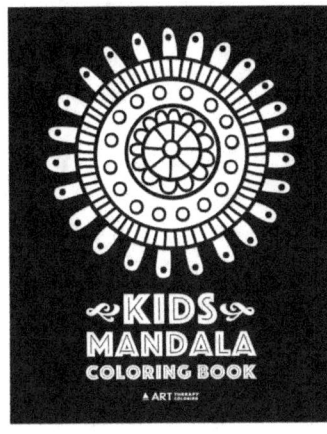

KIDS
MANDALA
COLORING BOOK

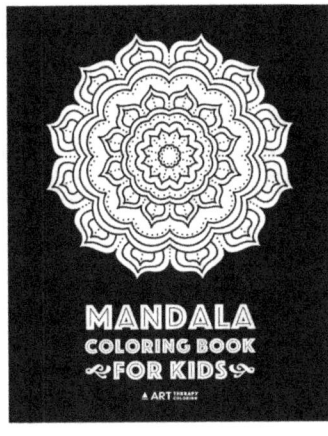

MANDALA
COLORING BOOK
FOR KIDS

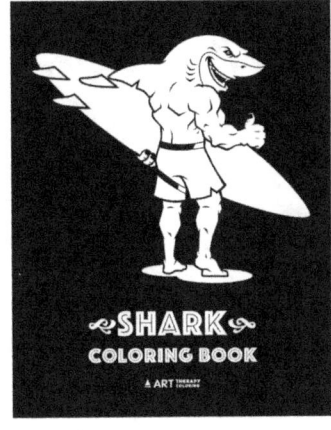

SHARK
COLORING BOOK

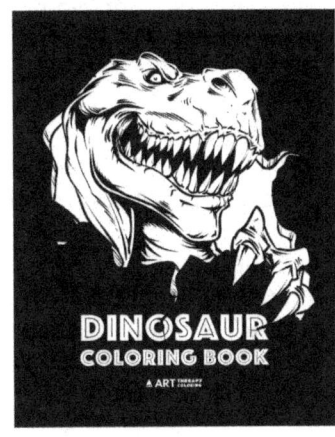

DINOSAUR
COLORING BOOK

Coloring Books For Special Occasions

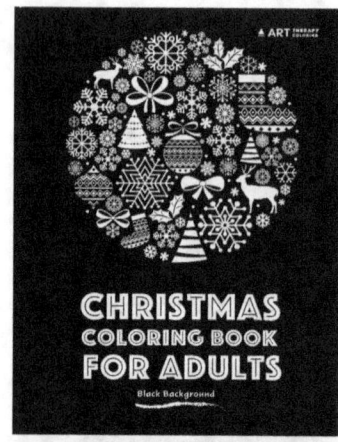

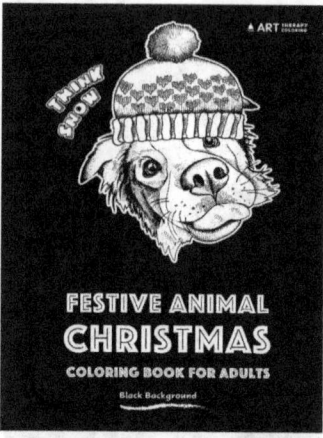

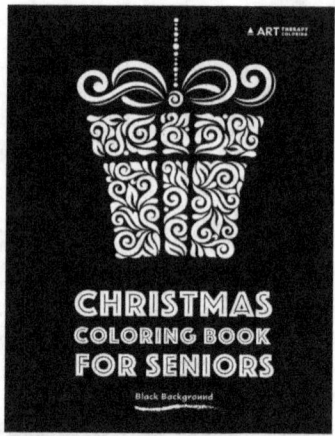

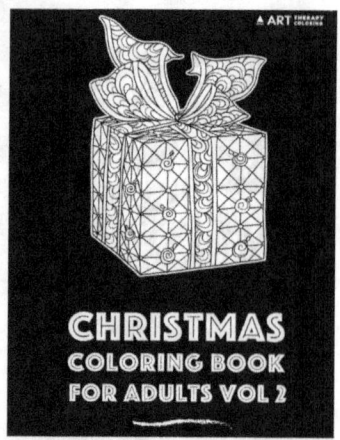

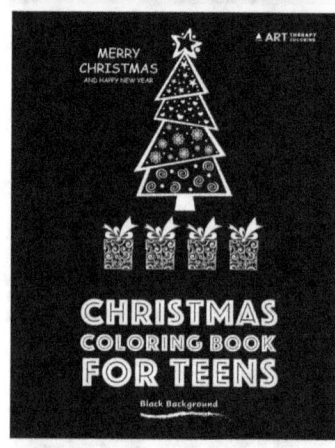

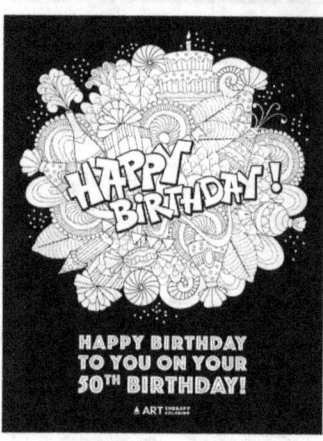

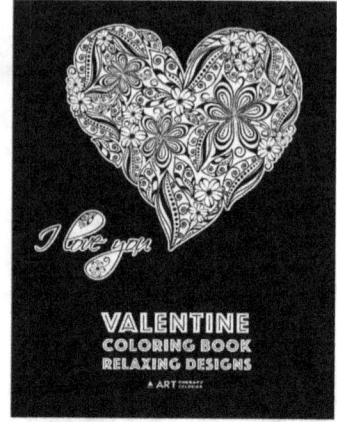

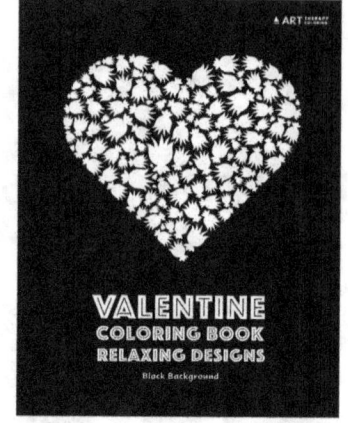

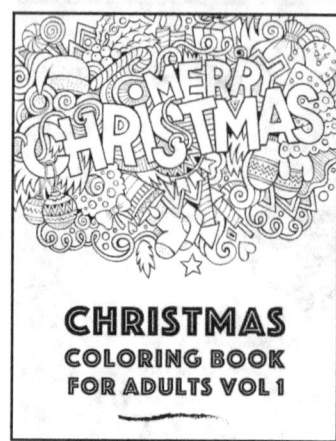

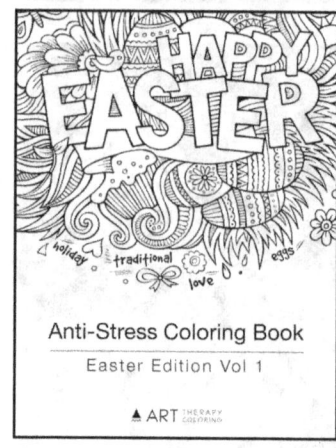

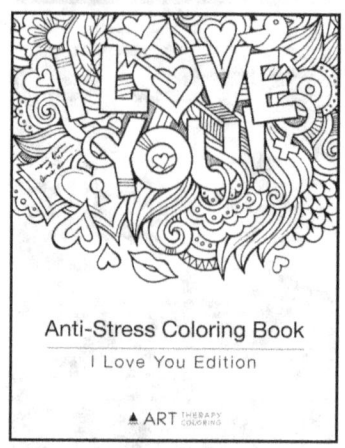

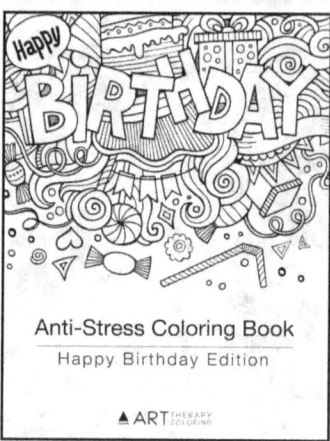

Coloring Books For Women
Relaxing Designs

Published by:
Art Therapy Coloring
El Dorado Hills, California
www.arttherapycoloring.com

Shutterstock Images

ISBN: 978-1-64126-062-6

www.ingramcontent.com/pod-product-compliance
Lightning Source LLC
Chambersburg PA
CBHW081343180526
45171CB00006B/593

* 9 7 8 1 6 4 1 2 6 0 6 2 6 *